For Stephen Card, generous friend and master artist.

Passenger Liners
French Style

by
William H. Miller

Published by
Carmania Press

Unit 212, Station House, 49, Greenwich High Road, London, SE10 8JL, Great Britain.

© William H. Miller and Carmania Press.
ISBN 0 9534291 7 2   First published 2001.
British Library Cataloguing for Publication Data.
A Catalogue Record for this book is available from the British Library.

Edited by Dennis Stonham.
Artwork production by Alan Kittridge.
Printed by The Amadeus Press, Ltd., Cleckheaton, West Yorkshire.

Contents

FRONT COVER: **Stephen Card's nostalgic painting of the great *Ile de France* in her post-War form with two, more modern funnels.** *Stephen Card, from the Tom Cassidy Collection.*

INSIDE FRONT COVER: **In this artistic view by Moran Towing Company's photographer, dated August 17th, 1955, three company tugs are among those poised to assist the impressive *Liberté* into the north slip of Pier 88.** *Moran Towing & Transportation Co.*

REAR COVER: **A striking view of the *France* at Southampton during one of her transatlantic voyages.** *Richard Faber Collection.*

Acknowledgements

These ocean liner books would not be possible if it were not for the great generosity of many friends, other acquaintances and numerous companies and organizations. Through them, and with their photographs and recollections, these ships return to life. And they are portrayed for future generations, the younger enthusiasts and historians. I am especially grateful to the amazing Anthony Cooke and his Carmania Press for creating so many splendid books in recent years and thereby adding to the fascinating history of passenger ships. Warmest appreciation and highest praises go also to Ernest Arroyo, the keeper of the late Frank Cronican's photo collection, to the extraordinary Frank Braynard, to the endlessly generous Richard Faber and to the great collectors like Eric Johnson and Hisashi Noma. Of course, special thanks go to the brilliant Stephen Card. His art adds so much to the covers of these books. Der Scutt's fine drawing of the *France* also enhances this book. And I must also thank Claude Molteni de Villermont for contributing his evocative foreword.

Other photographer-collector friends include Marius Bar, Michael Cassar, Luís Miguel Correia, Frank Duffy, Alex Duncan, Laurence Dunn, Peter T. Eisele, Gerhard Fiebiger, Andres Hernandez, Arnold Kludas, Michael D. J. Lennon, Jacques Letard, Richard K. Morse, Ove Nielsen, John O'Leary, Robert Pelletier, Fred Rodriguez, Antonio Scrimali, James Shaw, Roger Sherlock, Steffen Weirauch and Victor Young.

Companies and other organizations that have assisted include the Costa Line, Flying Camera Inc., French Line, Hapag-Lloyd Shipyard, Med Sun Lines, Moran Towing & Transportation Company, North German Lloyd, the Port Authority of Le Havre, the Port Authority of New York & New Jersey and the World Ship Society.

And last, but hardly least, my special thanks go to Abe Michaelson, my business partner, to Tom Greene and to my family.

Introduction

During the 1950s and into the early 1960s, as my fascination and deep interest grew, my love of ocean liners took hold. Dozens of shipping lines, not only at New York, but at London, Rotterdam, Marseilles, Genoa, Trieste and even distant Hong Kong, Singapore and Sydney, had passenger services that spanned the globe. My interest in world geography deepened, my sense of history expanded. Britain, for example, still had many of her colonial outposts and these required shipping services, often passenger ship links. Even some of the former colonial connections persisted, such as Holland with Indonesia and the Italians with parts of East Africa. In other ways, the West Germans had strong trading patterns with the Far East, as did the Italians with South America and the Dutch with South Africa.

An aunt of mine worked in the old Cunard Building, number 25 along New York City's Lower Broadway, but on an upper floor and for the Marine Department of what was then a great and thriving railroad, the New York Central. Still a schoolboy, I received monthly deliveries of maritime magazines, which had been read and then stacked in the New York Central offices. Copies of the likes of the *Maritime Reporter, Marine News & Engineering, Towline, Via Port of New York* and others found their way onto my little bedroom desk. But occasionally, I'd have a special treat: an updated copy of the *Official Steamship & Airways Guide*. This had almost biblical significance for me. From A-to-Z, it listed almost every noted steamship line in the World, their addresses (to which I often sent letters requesting brochures, deck plans and even postcards) and, most interesting of all, consolidated sailing schedules of major liners. Therefore, not only did I have a bird's eye view of the nearby likes of the Cunard, Italian and United States lines but also the far-away, often exotic types such as American President, Lloyd Triestino, Mitsui-OSK, P&O-Orient, Royal Interocean and Union-Castle.

Many hours, both after school and during the summer holidays, were spent reading and re-reading these lists. Sometimes, in deep imagination and colorful fantasy from riverside Hoboken, I plotted trips, often long ones, with connections at varied ports along the way and usually on very interesting ships – the *Orsova, Iberia, Arundel Castle, Asia, Giulio Cesare* and *Tegelberg* among them. I even tried to create trips around the World that fitted within the dates of the ten-week summer holiday from school.

Before Laurence Dunn's extraordinary *Passenger Liners*, that thick, beautifully produced, fact-filled first edition of 1959, some of the smaller companies, their services and their ships were unknown to me. I took that 474-page volume to the New Jersey beaches so often during our summer excursions that the salt air caused the binding to dry out. (I've since gotten a second, replacement copy.) No book or author was a better teacher or guide about worldwide passenger ships in those busy, long-ago years.

The British passenger fleet was the largest back then, of course, but many other flags were fascinating as well. I particularly liked the French. In a rough estimate, there were some fifty French passenger ships in worldwide services. The Compagnie Générale Transatlantique, the French Line to me, was, of course, the biggest and the most familiar. In those years before the giant *France* entered service in 1962, CGT had three splendid liners on their luxury run in and out of New York – the celebrated *Liberté*, the beloved *Ile de France* and the smallish but handsome *Flandre*. They also ran a Caribbean passenger service, worked by the pre-War *Colombie* and the *Flandre*'s near sister, the *Antilles*. But less known, at least to American travellers, armchair-type or otherwise, were CGT's two African runs – one from Bordeaux to Casablanca on the west coast; the other, shorter but busier, to North Africa – to Algeria and Tunisia – out of Marseilles. There was even one further passenger service – from Marseilles as well as Nice over to nearby Corsica.

But I was equally fascinated by the Marseilles-based Messageries Maritimes. In the late '50s, they had no less than a dozen passenger ships plying several far-flung routes: Europe to the Far East via Suez; to East Africa and the Indian Ocean via Suez; and, longest of all, to the South Pacific and Australia via the Caribbean and Panama. MM, as it was abbreviated, also ran a "short sea" passenger service between Australia and the New Hebrides.

There was also Chargeurs Réunis, who carried passengers on three routes: to the East Coast of South America, to West Africa and out to Southeast Asia. Transports Maritimes also ran to South America and Cie. Paquet, Fraissinet-Fabre and Cie. Mixte all had routes to Africa. I wrote to all of them and received replies, often in French. There were color brochures from Messageries Maritimes, a book of their history from Paquet and oversized, tissue-paper, pull-out deck plans from Fabre.

But, sadly, in these forty or so years, they have all gone. I corresponded in the late '60s with Ted Scull, the well-known passenger ship writer and cruise journalist. He was living in London at the time and, in letters that bounced back and forth across the Atlantic, we shared the latest passenger ship news and even the flash rumours. The passenger ship industry was then in the deep throes of change, consolidation, withdrawal. Sometimes, Ted would send figures, the numbers of passengers arriving at various North European ports. I still have some of these. Clearly, many of the liners were running at only 50% of their capacities, others lower still. Those numbers told a great deal. Passenger ships on those long-distance services, the "blue water routes" as they were sometimes called, were in their final decline. The airlines were now the preferred way to go.

With a spark of intuition, I managed a trip across the Atlantic, 5 days from New York to Le Havre via Southampton, on the extraordinary *France*. It was July 1973, the next-to-her-last summer season. But we did not know that. Fifteen months later, in October 1974, she was gone forever, her French life terminated by merciless Government cuts in the subsidies on which that great ship depended. Matters were sealed when the crew protested

and demanded as much as a 35% increase in their wages. Started in 1855, CGT/French Line's transatlantic liner service had ended. By then, almost all the other ships mentioned in these pages no longer flew the Tricolor. They were all gone. Later, I managed sailings (cruises, actually) in the former *Flandre*, then called the *Carla C.*, and aboard the ex-*Cambodge*, then the *Stella Solaris*. But both had been heavily refitted and so there was barely a trace of their Gallic heritage.

I went to St. Nazaire in April 1984, to the big Chantiers de l'Atlantique shipyard. After a long gap in building passenger ships, the yard had managed something of a comeback with two superb sisters for the Holland America Line, the 33,900-ton *Nieuw Amsterdam* and *Noordam*. Unquestionably, they were two of the best decorated ships of their time. We sailed up to Le Havre on the *Noordam* and later made a celebratory cruise across the mid-Atlantic to the Azores, Bermuda and finally to Tampa. At Le Havre during our stopover, I recall seeing the great passenger terminals. They were all but completely boarded up and high weeds grew among the tracks where the boat trains once ran. In earlier days departures were great occasions, but now only a handful of well-wishers saw us off on that warm Sunday evening.

I was back at St. Nazaire three years later, in April 1987, for the "floating out" of what was then the World's largest passenger ship, the 73,000-ton *Sovereign of the Seas*. There was a luncheon at the yard. Great photos of bygone French liners peered down upon us. During an impromptu tour afterward, we saw the desolate slip where the mighty *France* had been created more than thirty years before and a single, older crane, long since displaced but kept on as something of a museum-piece from the days of refitting the *Ile de France* and overhauling the *Liberté*.

During another visit to Le Havre, on a summer's day in 1994, I came across the vast CGT archives now stored in the very pierside buildings that once welcomed the great liners. The collection is an Aladdin's Cave of photos, artworks, paper items, glass and china and silver, and many of those magnificent company models. Hopefully, many books will come out of this brilliant collection.

Because there is now only a handful of French-owned deep sea passenger ships, I felt that the entire magnificent French passenger fleet, beginning with the end of the Second World War and concentrating on the 1950s, deserved one more, loving look. It comes out as an impressive collection – the *Liberté* and the *Antilles*, the *Louis Lumère* and the *Henri Poincaré*, the *Cambodge* and *Félix Roussel*, the *Fred Scamaroni* and the *Nossi-Be*, the exotic *Sidi-Okba* and *Sidi-Bel-Abbes* and *El Djezaïr*.

In imagination, I can see it clearly: a foggy day at Le Havre – the *Ile de France* and the *Colombie* are in port, the *Lavoisier* is arriving from South America while the *Charles Tellier* is loading. A foghorn, dockside activity, perhaps a midnight sailing, the drama of the French!

Bill Miller,
Secaucus, New Jersey,
January, 2001.

4

Foreword

When Bill Miller told me that he intended to devote his new book to the French passenger ships and asked me to write a small preface, I was delighted and honoured. I had read with great interest his book on the Italian liners and had recognised the qualities of this well-known writer.

I was equally happy to have the excuse to re-live my career as a maritime agent, starting 40 years ago as a booking clerk in a Parisian travel agency. I recall the 'grande époque' of the French liners – the departure of the trains from the Gare Saint Lazare amid crowds of excited journalists, the flash of cameras, the piles of Vuitton luggage, the sprays of flowers thrust upon stars of show-business, the arts and politics – Marlene Dietrich, Helena Rubinstein, Hemingway, Yehudi Menhuin, Clark Gable, Marcel Cerdan and a myriad others.

I also remember the arrival, two hours later, at the Gare Maritime at Le Havre and the sight of a great ship with its vast black hull, white superstructure and enormous red and black funnels (the famous Transat red) – the *Ile de France* or the *Liberté* or the *France*.

But, thanks to Bill Miller's book, I am also reminded of the blue Mediterranean sky of Marseille (the port of the East, as we say in French) and the line of impeccably white Messageries Maritimes ships – perhaps the *Laos, Cambodge, Félix Roussel, Maréchal Joffre*. Then there were the beautiful Algerian packets of the Compagnie de Navigation Mixte moored at the quays of La Joliette. One could also see the black funnels and light grey hulls of the ships of the Compagnie Paquet serving the West African coast. Memories flood back, too, of the port of Bordeaux and the departure for South America or for distant parts of Africa of the vessels of the Chargeurs Réunis. The passenger lists included many priests, not to mention the overseas administrators and their turbulent children.

Of course, as a director of a maritime company, I have had occasion to know other aspects of the French ports and very different departures, but thanks to this book I remember precisely the so elegant look of the French liners of yesterday which served our vast colonial empire. The independence of those far-off countries and the arrival of a new competitor, the aeroplane, put an end to this style of travel.

My thanks go to Bill Miller who has assembled in this nostalgic book many rare photographs in black and white and numerous anecdotes, souvenirs of our maritime past from a time when smoke still rose from the funnels of the French liners. C'était le bon vieux temps.

Claude Molteni de Villermont,
Courbevoie, France.

MESSAGERIES MARITIMES

sur tous les océans..
pour tous les continents

1
Compagnie Générale Transatlantique

There used to be a publicity slogan, "More seagulls follow the French Line ships than any others because the scraps of food are better". For almost all its days, the company was known for its splendid cuisine as well as its grand service and glamorous luxury. They had some of the very finest liners ever to go to sea. Later, it was quite rightly said that one of their ships, the celebrated *Ile de France*, had such enormous style and ambiance that she alone put the "bon" in "bon voyage".

With origins as far back as 1855, the company – with the full blessing of the French government – started sailing ship services to New York as well as to eastern Canada and the Caribbean. It soon began running steamships and expanded steadily. Increasingly, it brought new standards of luxury to ocean travel. *La Normandie* of 1883, for example, was the first Atlantic liner to be equipped with interior plumbing. Thereafter, the Atlantic voyager would see no more of that early morning ritual of cabin stewards emptying chamber pots over the lee rail!

The four-funnelled, 23,000-ton *France* of 1912 was the first super-liner in French Line annals and she led to a series of progressively larger and finer ships: the *Paris*, the aforementioned *Ile de France* and finally the sumptuous 83,423-ton *Normandie* of 1935. To this day, many consider her to have been the most luxurious ocean liner ever built. Filled with the likes of Lalique fixtures, Aubusson carpets and even cages filled with live birds in her Winter Garden, she was every bit a 'floating Hollywood'. Tragically, she saw only four years of commercial service before burning at her New York pier in the winter of 1942.

The French Line kept its Atlantic service going until as late as 1974. Then the all-important government subsidies went instead to Concorde. Their last ship was the 1,035-foot *France*, the longest liner yet built and a ship that at least one critic called "the best French restaurant in the World". Today, she is the greatly rebuilt *Norway*.

The French Line remains, but as the CGM, the Compagnie Générale Maritime, and only in the cargo trades.

The instantly recognisable shape of the last French superliner, *France*, is caught in this attractive drawing by Der Scutt. *Der Scutt.*

Normandie.

The *Normandie* does not really come within the scope of this book, which deals primarily with French passenger ships that sailed after the Second World War, particularly in the late 1950s. But, as Frank Braynard reminds us, there was a rumor after the War – a very slight and perhaps far-fetched one – that the great *Normandie* would be rebuilt, in smaller form, for a return to service. Her Russian designer, Vladimir Yourkevitch, proposed to the U.S. Maritime Commission, by then the owners of the former French flagship, that she could be rebuilt as a medium-sized liner. Nothing came of his devoted proposal but it gives us an excuse to include this grandest of ships in our book.

The 1,028-foot long *Normandie* was, in fact, still afloat, albeit only as a mud-stained, fire-scarred hull, in 1946. Her former owners, the Compagnie Générale Transatlantique, the French Line to Americans, were then busily planning their return to North Atlantic luxury service. With the proud *Ile de France* still on government duty as a trooper, the start-up would be subdued at best. The sole available survivor, a long way from the extravagant size and standard of the 83,423-ton *Normandie*, was the 19,900-ton *De Grasse*. Meanwhile, the *Normandie* lay at Brooklyn, salvaged and awaiting Washington's final verdict on her fate. Here, the $60,000,000 liner is shown in grander days, sailing from Manhattan's Pier 88 on September 28th 1938. *Cronican-Arroyo Collection.*

The *Normandie*, the World's largest as well as fastest ship for a time, had been completed in the spring of 1935. On her maiden voyage, she took the prized Blue Riband with a speed of just short of 30 knots and remained headline news thereafter. Her exceptional exterior, capped by three large, progressively raked funnels, was just a hint of the grandeur and innovation within. She was certainly the most extravagantly decorated liner of her day, possibly of all time. The main Dining Room, for example, was fitted out in hammered glass and bronze and highlighted by Lalique fixtures. It was, as French Line publicity material never failed to remind interested readers, slightly longer than the Hall of Mirrors at Versailles, rose three decks in height and sat 1,000 guests. The Theatre was

the first ever fitted to a liner and the indoor pool was 80 feet of graduating water levels. The Winter Garden included exotic birds in cages and sprays of water, and the Main Lounge was covered in Dupas panels, while Aubusson tapestries were used to upholster the chairs. Every First Class suite and stateroom had a different décor. But commercial life was tragically short for the great *Normandie*. In little more than four years, on August 28th l939, she was 'temporarily' laid up at Pier 88 due to the threat of war in Europe. She would never sail again. On December 12th 1941, five days after the attack on Pearl Harbor, she was taken over by the U.S. government. On the 24th, she was handed over to the U.S. Navy and renamed *USS Lafayette*. In this photograph, the large gold letters of her illustrious name are about to be removed by a shipyard crew on a cold, late December morning. *Cronican-Arroyo Collection.*

The conversion of the *Normandie* into the *USS Lafayette* took place at pierside and was entrusted to shipyard crews from Brooklyn and Hoboken. She was to be turned into a mighty, 15,000-plus capacity trooper

and was tentatively scheduled to sail for Boston on about February 14th 1942 (and then all the way to Australia via the South African Cape). A sense of urgency surrounded the entire project at the dockside at the foot of West 48th Street in Manhattan. Then, on February 9th, sparks from a workman's acetylene torch ignited a pile of kapok lifejackets. The fire spread quickly on that bitterly cold afternoon. Work crews evacuated the ship and firefighting units, both ashore and afloat, arrived at the scene. Suddenly, a thick blanket of orange-brown smoke spread over midtown Manhattan. *Cronican-Arroyo Collection.*

But the excitement led to miscalculation: while the fire itself created considerable damage, the firefighters were overzealous in pouring tons of water into the smouldering ship. In the early, still darkened hours of the next day, the giant *Normandie* capsized, unable to bear the weight of water within the hull.
Cronican-Arroyo Collection.

On her side, the *Normandie* presented the most difficult salvage job ever. Her funnels, masts and upper decks had to be slowly and systematically removed by floating cranes as great pumps simultaneously sucked harbor water out of that vast, burnt-out hulk. This extraordinary operation, which cost $5million, was completed in the late summer of 1943. The ship was finally righted, amid rumor and speculation that she would be rebuilt as an aircraft carrier. *Cronican-Arroyo Collection.*

Stripped and without power, the former *Normandie* was towed along the Hudson by a flotilla of tugs on November 3rd 1943. At that point, there were still confident reports that she would be refitted for service with the U.S. Navy. *Cronican-Arroyo Collection.*

The hull of the *Normandie* was laid-up in Brooklyn, at the extended Columbia Street pier, for some two years. There was continued talk of future plans. But as the War ended, the U.S. Navy passed title over to the Maritime Commission, who had no use for the ship. In October 1946, she was sold to a local New York harbor scrap metals firm and, a month later, she was towed to Port Newark, New Jersey for final dismantling. This extravagant ship of genius realized a mere $161,000 in the end. Within twelve months only her memory and her legend remained.

In this view, dated May 20th 1947, she was being demolished at the rate of 6-10 railroad carloads of scrap per day. Looking down from one of the large cranes, we have a bird's eye view of the debris-littered decks. The news agency caption to this photograph concluded with the words "crews of burners with glittering torches are slowly cutting the great ship into nothingness".

Cronican-Arroyo Collection.

Oregon.

When the Second World War ended in 1945, none of the French Line's big pre-War transatlantic liners was available to re-start the New York service. In order to commence sailings as soon as possible, the company had to use a much more modest ship. She was the 7,706-ton *Oregon* which had been built by the Bremer Vulkan yard at Vegesack in Germany in 1929. A cargo liner with 38 all-First Class passenger berths (later enlarged to 76), she had been designed especially for French Line's alternative transatlantic service, from Le Havre via Panama to the North

American Pacific coast. She was one of four sisters, the others being the *Washington*, *Wisconsin* and *Wyoming*. Used by the Allies during the War, she was pressed into commercial service just as the War in Europe ended, in May 1945. With those 76 passenger berths, she restarted French Line's Le Havre – New York service. She continued to sail, together with the *Wisconsin* and, later, the liner *De Grasse*, until the fall of 1948. Messageries Maritimes took her in 1950 and refitted her for their Marseilles – New Caledonia service via Panama with 184 berths in First Class and a certificate for a further 66 deck passengers. Later, she was converted to a hospital ship for service out in troubled Indo-China. She was sold in 1955 to Hong Kong buyers, who used a Panama flag for a concern known as Compañía Maritima Asiatic Panamense. She was renamed *Pacific Harmony*. But this phase of her life was all too brief. Later that same year, she grounded and became a total loss at **Murmugão**. *E. N. Taylor, Eric Johnson Collection.*

Wisconsin.

The 473-foot long *Wisconsin*, also built by Bremer Vulkan for the North Pacific route, was returned to CGT after extended American service during the War. She was handed over in the fall of 1945 and immediately restored. She too was given enlarged quarters for 76 one-class passengers. That December, she began sailing between Le Havre and New York (with occasional extensions to Philadelphia). She went on the Gulf of Mexico run in the fall of 1948 and then, three years later, was sold to the Polish Ocean Lines, becoming their *Fryderyk Chopin*. That name was changed to *Kaszuby* in 1957. She was converted to a fishing fleet 'mother ship' in 1961 and, in deepening old age, became the *Kapitan Maciejewicz* in 1973. Afterward, she became a schoolship at Landskrona in Sweden before being broken-up in May 1982. *E. N. Taylor, Eric Johnson Collection.*

De Grasse.

Built by Cammell Laird at Birkenhead, near Liverpool in England, the 574-foot long *De Grasse* had been a French Line Cabin Class intermediate liner in the 1920s and 1930s. One of the finest ships of this kind, she was used mainly on the North Atlantic route between Le Havre and New York, but without the great cachet and popular following enjoyed by the express liners. Although she had the fine décor to be expected of a French Line ship and the high standards of service and cuisine, nobody could have foreseen that by 1945 she would be one of France's largest ships and that two years later she would singlehandedly restore CGT's luxury service to New York.

The *De Grasse* had returned to home waters in the fall of 1939. In her original guise, with her pair of quite ordinary, upright stacks, she is seen here arriving at New York in October 1939, before heading back to France and lay-up at Bordeaux. She fell into Nazi hands and was used by them as an accommodation ship, never leaving her moorings for almost five years. But in their retreat, on August 30th 1944, the Nazi forces sank her. *Cronican-Arroyo Collection.*

The *De Grasse* was salvaged on August 30th 1945, exactly one year to the day after being scuttled. She was immediately brought to St. Nazaire for post-War refitting. The French Line took the opportunity not only of upgrading and modernizing her interiors (now reshaped for 664 passengers in all – 220 in First Class and 444 in Tourist), but also of changing her external appearance, giving her a new single stack with a rakish tilt. We see her here, with her transformation well underway, on March 18th 1947.
Cronican-Arroyo Collection.

Proudly, the 16-knot *De Grasse* steamed into New York harbor on July 25th 1947. The New York Times reported, "She is the first full passenger vessel of the French Line to come here in peacetime style since nearly eight years ago when her country went to war against Nazism. Dressed brightly from stem to stern with signal flags, she received a raucous welcome as she moved up the bay from Quarantine to her North River pier. At her welcoming reception, champagne corks popped and photographers' flash bulbs flared aboard the 23-year old liner." Here we see her on a later occasion, being assisted by a Moran tug. For two years, the *De Grasse* maintained the Le Havre – New York service with two passenger-freighters, the *Oregon* and the *Wisconsin*.
Cronican-Arroyo Collection.

In a busy dockside scene at Le Havre in 1951, the *De Grasse* is being worked by cranes between her crossings to and from New York. The bow of the *Colombie* can be seen just to the left. *Richard Faber Collection.*

The French Line had, of course, this extraordinary reputation for luxurious, highly stylized, almost over-the-edge décor, from the 1930s in particular. Fortunately, some artworks and furniture were kept in wartime storages. Some of them reappeared in the late 1940s and 1950s. The *De Grasse*'s First Class restaurant was a very attractive room, two decks high and columned, that recaptured something of the pre-War CGT ambiance. It remained untouched when the *De Grasse* became Canadian Pacific's *Empress of Australia* in the spring of 1953. *Richard Faber Collection.*

In 1952, with the *Ile de France* and *Liberté* restored and the new *Flandre* expected, the *De Grasse* was moved into the West Indies trade, sailing from Le Havre and Southampton. She was then in company with another pre-War CGT liner, the *Colombie* of 1931. It was a short-lived partnership, however, since the *De Grasse* was replaced by the brand new *Antilles* and so was placed on the sales lists. She found a buyer immediately. Canadian Pacific Steamships had just lost their pre-War *Empress of Canada* and, with a surge in traffic expected because of the Coronation in London that June, the *De Grasse* was the perfect and immediate replacement. In quick time, in April 1953, the French Tricolor was lowered and the British Red Ensign hoisted. Renamed *Empress of Australia*, the veteran ship began sailing between Montreal, Quebec City, Greenock and Liverpool. *Cronican-Arroyo Collection.*

She was sold again, in February 1956, to the Fratelli Grimaldi, Italian shipowners who specialized in older, converted passenger ships, primarily for low-fare migrant and tourist service. Renamed *Venezuela*, she was assigned to a more mid-Atlantic service now – sailing from Naples, Genoa and Cannes to the Caribbean and Venezuela. In 1960, she underwent an extensive rebuilding. A new, flared bow was fitted, increasing her length to 614 feet; and her passenger capacity was greatly enlarged to 1,480 in total – 180 in First Class, 500 in Tourist and 800 in Third Class. Unfortunately, on March 17th 1962, she stranded on the rocks at Cannes. Damaged and considered too old to repair, she was sent to Italian scrappers at La Spezia that summer. It was the end for one of the most enduring French Line passenger ships.
Antonio Scrimali.

The Fabulous Ile de France

The *Ile de France*, universally acknowledged as one of the greatest of all liners, had been a sensation when she entered service in 1927. She was neither the biggest nor the fastest, but she was distinguished by her interiors which were a startling break with the traditional styles and introduced a new chic to the North Atlantic. She immediately attracted 'the smart set' and continued to be a great success even after the French Line introduced their even more sensational *Normandie*.

Her wartime career as an Allied trooper was heroic, busy but exhausting. Under the watchful eye of managers P&O and then Cunard-White Star, the gray-hulled three-stacker, with her capacity upped to no less than 9,706 from the 1939 level of 1,586, sailed the North Atlantic, visited Cape Town and Sydney, voyaged across the Pacific and the Indian Ocean, passed through Suez and called at Marseilles, St. Nazaire and Cherbourg. In 1946, she was awarded the Croix de Guerre, France's highest military honor, usually only given to the most gallant men and women.

Le Havre was, of course, her homeport and the Maritime Station there was rebuilt after the bombers' devastation in an extraordinary nine months. It was ready for the *Ile* and her post-War debut in the summer of 1949, after a two-year stay at her builders' yard at St. Nazaire. A few days later, spraying fireboats, tooting tugs, flag-dressed ferries and even a blimp welcomed her back to New York and to her old berth, at Pier 88, West 48th Street. "Here is a romantic ship, a very romantic ship," wrote passenger liner connoisseur C. M. Squarey after seeing her at Southampton a few weeks later. "This ship is so utterly and superbly French that one scarcely dares to talk, or write, about her in other than the French language."

Her kitchens were once again flawless. One reporter said enthusiastically that no restaurant in Paris was better. Even in Tourist Class the food was outstanding. "We had skate in a delicious butter sauce at breakfast," recalled a 1951 Tourist Class passenger.

Celebrities like Rita Hayworth, Cary Grant and, naturally, Maurice Chevalier crossed on her in the 1950s. Occasionally, in deep winter, she would go cruising to the sunny Caribbean isles. Her biggest headlines came,

Launched at St. Nazaire on March 14th 1926, the *Ile de France* was one of the very great Atlantic liners. Designed as a somewhat larger, more extravagant, certainly more innovative version of the *Paris* of 1921, the *Ile* did, however, copy her exterior style rather closely. She too had three quite conventional stacks. *Cronican-Arroyo Collection.*

During the War, the *Ile de France*, then 43,450 tons, was under British control, managed as a troopship at first by P&O and then by Cunard-White Star. In this view, she is arriving at Honolulu on November 19th 1942. *Cronican-Arroyo Collection.*

perhaps, in 1956, when she went to the aid of the stricken Italian liner *Andrea Doria* after her collision with Sweden's *Stockholm*. Bound for Europe on that foggy summer's night of July 25th, the *Ile* changed course and sped to the scene of the accident. Standing by, she later took on 753 survivors. Eric Meyer was aboard the *Ile* at the time and recalled, "While a few of us were lingering over drinks in the lounge late that night, word spread that we were called to an emergency by an SOS. We arrived at 1.45 a.m. The sight of the *Ile* looming through the fog, with her two great

red and black stacks floodlit and her name spelled out in electric lights along the top deck, must have been a tremendous boost to the survivors waiting to be rescued. She was an omen of hope." Later, she led the procession of gallant ships bringing the survivors into New York harbor.

Economics, the airlines and pure old age spelled the end for the 792-foot long *Ile* in the fall of 1958. In the fading light of a November afternoon, she left New York on her farewell passage. "There were tears. It was very emotional," said a French Line employee who stood to the very end on the open-air verandah at the tip of Pier 88 to wave her off. "She still looked so grand, so majestic. Those great whistles screeched into the melancholy autumn air. But it was more than the passing of a ship, it was the passing of an era – the 1920s and 1930s, extravagant design and innovative décor, Art Deco on the high seas, film stars and steamer trunks."

"It was always harder to diet on the *Ile de France* than on any other ship," noted Lewis Gordon, who crossed often in her. Another American passenger added, "I don't know of a French ship that isn't good – they don't know how to spoil good food. And the *Ile* was the very best."

After a brief duty as a prop in the Hollywood disaster film, *The Last Voyage*, the 32-year old liner was dismantled by the Japanese at Osaka. Demolition was completed by September 1959.

The 791-foot long ship was handed back to the French Line in February 1946. For a time, she ran Cherbourg – New York austerity sailings as well as some trooping voyages to Indo-China. Her post-War refit began at St. Nazaire in April 1947 and took over two years. Among other changes, the original three funnels were removed and replaced by two rather more modern ones. *Richard Faber Collection.*

Triumph for the French: thoroughly refitted, the glorious *Ile de France* returns to New York on her post-War maiden voyage. The date is July 27th 1949. The two wider funnels have given the great ship an entirely different look. *Cronican-Arroyo Collection.*

As part of her post-War 'maiden year', the *Ile de France* called at Boston's Commonwealth Pier on Columbus Day, October 12th 1949. It was the 23-knot liner's first call there since before the War and she was the biggest passenger ship to sail from that New England port since 1939. *Cronican-Arroyo Collection.*

The famous First Class Dining Room was redesigned after the War, but retained that classic French Line feature, a grand staircase as entrance. The cuisine remained beyond compare and, as usual with the French Line, the wines were free. Two private dining rooms were forward of this main room. *Cronican-Arroyo Collection.*

The First Class Smoking Room, located on the Promenade Deck, was especially created for card games, conversation or, as the company suggested, "a leisurely read of *L'Atlantique*, the French-English newspaper published daily aboard ship". The wall panels, on the left and right, came from the *Normandie*.
Cronican-Arroyo Collection.

The First Class Entrance Hall included a central seating area and shops placed along the outer edges. With its modish stairwell, this space had much of a 1930s Manhattan skyscraper feel about it. *Cronican-Arroyo Collection.*

The theatre – the largest yet fitted to a French Line ship – was used for both films and stage performances. It had a seating capacity of 350. Films were shown several times each day, but at different times for First Class and for Cabin Class passengers. *Cronican-Arroyo Collection.*

After the War, the *Ile*'s capacity was revised to 541 in First Class, 577 in Cabin Class and 227 in Tourist Class. Minimum summer season First Class fares started at $350 per person for the 7-day crossing to either Southampton or Plymouth and Le Havre. The Versailles Suite, shown here in two views, was one of a dozen de luxe apartments located on the Main Deck. Although the suite was created to sleep two passengers, the handsomely appointed sitting room could accommodate two more and its folding doors could be pushed back to make one large room for entertaining. It was air-conditioned and included a telephone. The décor featured hand-woven carpets as well as French walnut furniture. *Cronican-Arroyo Collection.*

Another of the grand apartments, the Fontainebleau Suite (with bedroom and sitting area), was priced from $1,800 per person for a weeklong crossing. *Cronican-Arroyo Collection.*

Ile de France celebrity passengers in the early 1950s included singer Lena Horne, film star Rita Hayworth and His Serene Highness Prince Rainier of Monaco.

Richard Faber Collection.

The enclosed Promenade Deck included neatly placed rows of steamer chairs, each one with a monogrammed CGT cushion.
Cronican-Arroyo Collection.

The broad Boat Deck was a popular area for walking, deck games or a good book on a soft deck chair.
Richard Faber Collection.

The indoor pool was styled in a very simple moderne.
Cronican-Arroyo Collection.

Decorated by Le Bucheron, the Cabin Class Salon included a staircase of illuminated glass. This room was made even more magnificent by the large bay windows overlooking the forward part of the ship.
Cronican-Arroyo Collection.

French Line claimed that the same chefs in the same kitchens prepared food for the Cabin Class Restaurant as for the First Class. Cabin Class passengers, however, ate in rather less awe-inspiring surroundings. *Cronican-Arroyo Collection.*

A berth in this outside cabin for four in Cabin Class was priced from $250 per person for a peak summertime sailing in the mid-1950s. French Line advertised that Cabin Class was "more spacious and elaborate" than in pre-War days. *Cronican-Arroyo Collection.*

Chairs in the Tourist Class Restaurant were made of varnished makore mahogany. *Cronican-Arroyo Collection.*

Cabins in Tourist Class aboard the *Ile de France*, such as this inside double, lacked private bathroom facilities but had a washbasin. Tourist Class amenities included a Smoking Room and Bar, a Restaurant and separate outdoor deck space. A wintertime off-season sailing was priced from $170 per person in the 1950s. *Cronican-Arroyo Collection.*

The late Frank Cronican, third from the right in this group enjoying a pre-sailing drink in 1953, was a great friend to the French Line New York office, restoring many of the company's ship models and becoming an expert in the history of their fleet. *Cronican-Arroyo Collection.*

French Line passenger ships usually sailed from New York in the late morning, often at 11.30... but the occasional midnight sailing had, perhaps, a more dramatic feel. Here, the *Ile*'s thundering steam whistles signal that it is thirty minutes before her pre-lunchtime departure from Pier 88. Anyone not booked to travel should leave the ship. *Cronican-Arroyo Collection.*

On July 26th 1956, the *Ile de France* made headlines when she returned to New York with 753 survivors from the Italian liner *Andrea Doria* which had sunk after a collision with the Swedish *Stockholm* off Nantucket Island the night before. The beloved *Ile* became a "heroic ship" and was given a special rescue-at-sea award by the US Coast Guard. *Cronican-Arroyo Collection.*

After 31 years of service, and just as the jets were beginning their takeover on the North Atlantic, the *Ile de France* was retired. Amid emotional scenes, she departed from New York for the last time on November 10th, 1958. *Cronican-Arroyo Collection.*

Amidst rumors that she might become a floating hotel, or even a museum, the *Ile* was prepared for sale and for the auction of some of her furnishings. In this picture, canvas sheets have been spread over the central carpeting while overlays cover the chairs and sofas. On December 11th 1958, the ship was sold to Yamamoto & Company, scrap merchants of Osaka, Japan. This photograph is dated four days later.
Richard Faber Collection.

A sad winter's day, February 26th 1959, marked the departure of the *Ile de France* from her home port to the Far East for demolition. Renamed *Furanzu Maru* for the long, slow voyage (note the Japanese lettering on the stern), she finally reached Osaka on April 9th. Once there, however, she was leased to a Hollywood film studio at the rate of $4,000 a day, to be used as a floating prop in the disaster movie *The Last Voyage*, starring Robert Stack and Dorothy Malone. Under the fictional name *Claridon*, she was carefully scuttled in shallow waters off the Japanese coast. Afterward, she was pumped out and brought into Osaka for the inevitable scrapping. *Richard Faber Collection.*

The Charming Colombie

With her all-white hull and single funnel, tapered and painted in that distinctive French-red and black, the *Colombie* must have been a beautiful sight when seen against the blue of the Caribbean. She was the only pre-War built French liner still in the West Indies trade and was a great favorite for many years. She also made occasional European cruises. In all, she had quite a long life which included stints as a wartime trooper for the Allies and then as a hospital ship. Finally, she had a new career as a Greek-flag, Mediterranean-based cruiseship.

Launched at Dunkirk in July 1931, the 509-foot long *Colombie* was built with two rather ordinary stacks. She looked better, more original, in later years. She worked the Le Havre – West Indies trade until the outbreak of the War in September 1939. That summer, she had, in fact, made something of a detour – a three-week cruise to New York for the World's Fair.

At first laid-up for safety at Fort de France on Martinique, the *Colombie* went back to sea, but was taken by US forces at Casablanca in December 1942. Following her arrival at New York in early 1943, she was selected for conversion to a trooper with 2,638 berths. The work was completed by the following October. She operated under the auspices of the War Shipping Administration with the French Line serving as general agents. She left New York on her first trooping voyage, on October 21st, bound for Glasgow and other British ports. She then made other crossings between New York and the Clyde. She also sailed from New York and Norfolk to the Mediterranean, for Naples, Leghorn and Gibraltar. In December 1944, she was selected for conversion to a hospital ship.

Refitted to carry 828 patients, the *Colombie* was converted at a Brooklyn shipyard between January and April of 1945. She was renamed *USS Aleda E. Lutz*, honoring an Army nurse killed in a plane crash in southern France in November 1944 after having participated in 190 missions to evacuate wounded personnel by air. The ship set off for Europe on two separate trips, but then had further conversion work done at another Brooklyn shipyard, Todd's in the Erie Basin. Afterward, she set off for Manila via the Panama Canal but the voyage had to be discontinued at Honolulu due to main gearing problems.

In April 1946 she was back at New York, at the French Line's Pier 88, where she was officially returned to her owners. After some repairs, she then began sailing as a hospital ship to Indo-China for the French government.

In the meantime, to re-open their Caribbean service

The 509-foot long *Colombie* was commissioned in November 1931 especially for the Le Havre – West Indies service and for occasional cruising. She is seen here on a visit to Stockholm during a Baltic cruise. The year is 1935. *Cronican-Arroyo Collection.*

The 17-knot, 13,391 ton *Colombie* served as the US Army hospital ship *USS Aleda E. Lutz* for about a year, from April 1945 until April 1946. She is shown here in New York harbor on her first outward trip in medical service. *Ernest Arroyo Collection.*

Returned to the French and restored to her original name, the *Colombie* is seen here on May 23rd 1946 with her refit at the Bethlehem Steel shipyard at 56th Street in Brooklyn almost complete, but still wearing some of her US Army hospital ship markings. She sailed for Marseilles on May 29th and then proceeded to Indo-China for further hospital ship duties. *Cronican-Arroyo Collection.*

In 1948-50, the *Colombie* was rebuilt at De Schelde shipyard at Flushing in Holland. She was fitted with a new, single, tapered funnel. Her accommodations were restyled also – for 192 in First Class, 140 in Cabin and 246 in Tourist. In the mid-1950s, the 12-day voyage from Le Havre to Guadeloupe and Martinique in the French West Indies was priced from $300 in First Class, $230 in Cabin and $150 in Tourist. *Cronican-Arroyo Collection.*

the French Line had to use chartered tonnage, namely the 9,400-ton *Katoomba*, Greek-owned by the Goulandris group, which had been an Australian coastal passenger ship in her previous life. In addition, the 5,100-ton *George Washington* was bought from American owners after a career in the coastal trades and in occasional cruising and was renamed *Gascogne*. These ships were merely stop-gaps, however.

By November 1950, the greatly rebuilt *Colombie* was back in Caribbean service. She had been refitted at De Schelde shipyard at Flushing in Holland and had been given her new single stack and improved accommodations. C. M. Squarey particularly approved of the Winter Garden: "It is a room where the windows are well down to deck level and so permit visibility when reclining in the exceptionally comfortable, green-coloured garden chairs." He also liked the Dining Saloon which one entered down

an imposing stairway. The *Colombie* was, in fact, well received and sailed almost without competition.

Teamed from 1953 onwards with the larger *Antilles*, the 17-knot *Colombie* was generally routed from Le Havre and Southampton via Vigo to Pointe à Pitre, Roseau, Fort de France, St Lucia, Trinidad and Barbados (with periodic extensions to La Guaira, Curacao and Cartagena, and homewards, perhaps via Kingston). Fares by the early 1960s were listed as $350 in First Class, $248 in Cabin and $194 in Tourist.

When the *Flandre* was withdrawn from North Atlantic service, she joined her sister *Antilles* on the Caribbean run. In 1963, therefore, the old *Colombie* was displaced, made redundant and, very briefly, sent on some European cruises: Norway, the Mediterranean, etc. But she was soon to be found on the sales lists.

Greece's Typaldos Lines were busily expanding their

Eastern Mediterranean passenger and cruise fleets. Among others, they had acquired two American liners, the 9,100-ton *Santa Rosa* and *Santa Paula* of 1932. They sailed as the *Athinai* and *Acropolis*. Typaldos wanted a third, similar ship and so bought the *Colombie*, which they promptly renamed *Atlantica*. She was to have been chartered, in the summer of 1964, to the shortlived New York-based Caribbean Cruise Lines to sail on 7-day cruises down to Bermuda and Nassau. She was advertised as the *Atlantic*. But American Export Lines, who already owned a passenger ship named *Atlantic*, protested and threatened legal action. So Caribbean Cruise Lines simply changed the ship's advertised name to *Atlantic II*. Briefly, it was said that she might become the *Atlanticos* as an alternative. But soon, there were other problems, including too few bookings, and so the entire charter and schedule were cancelled. The ship remained in the Mediterranean as the

Atlantica and sailed mostly between Venice, Split, Piraeus, Limassol, Haifa, Larnaca, Rhodes and Piraeus before returning to Venice.

Typaldos soon fell on hard times. In December 1966, their ferry *Heraklion* sank in an Aegean storm with the loss of, it was thought, 241 lives – although the exact number was never known. In the court case which followed, the ship was found to have been unsafely loaded. One of the Typaldos brothers was sent to jail, but was later released on appeal. The firm was ruined and their ships were soon seized by the National Bank of Greece, who were the mortgage-holders. The *Atlantica*, among others, was sent to lay-up in Perama Bay, near Piraeus. She never sailed again. She was partly scrapped in 1970 and then the remaining hull was towed to Barcelona four years later for the final dismantling.

Gascogne

To assist temporarily on the Le Havre – Caribbean run, the French Line used the 5,184-ton *Gascogne* from 1949 until 1952. This 16-knot, 375-foot long ship had been built in 1924 at the Newport News shipyard in Virginia for the New York-based Old Dominion Line. As the *George Washington*, she sailed on the overnight run between New York and Norfolk. Later used by Eastern Steamship Lines and as a cruise ship for the Alcoa Steamship Company, she served briefly in Alaskan waters for shortlived Seattle owners in 1948. Soon thereafter, she was acquired by the French government and managed by CGT. In March 1952, no longer needed on the Caribbean run, she was transferred to Messageries Maritimes and participated in their long-haul service between Marseilles and Saigon via Suez. She was retired in the summer of 1955 and soon sold to Hong Kong breakers. *Eric Johnson Collection.*

Katoomba

While the *Colombie* was being rebuilt and modernized in Holland between 1948 and 1950, the French Line chartered the veteran 9,424-ton, Greek-owned *Katoomba*. She had been built back in 1913 by Harland & Wolff of Belfast as an Australian coastal passenger liner sailing between Sydney and Fremantle. Sold to the Goulandris group (the Greek Line) in 1946, but to a Panama-flag subsidiary, Compañia Maritima Del Este, she ran some Mediterranean – New York sailings (with accommodations for 52 in First Class and 754 in Tourist Class) before going on

charter to CGT, beginning in 1947. Renamed *Columbia*, she resumed her Greek Line sailings from 1950 until 1957, and was broken up in Japan two years later. *Alex Duncan.*

Gouverneur Général Chanzy

Besides the famed North Atlantic service to New York and the Caribbean service, the CGT also ran two other passenger lines – from Marseilles to North Africa and from Bordeaux to West Africa. These supported quite separate fleets of smaller, perhaps lesser known ships. The *Gouverneur Général Chanzy* was, by the mid-1950s, the veteran of these fleets and the last traditional twin-funnel French passenger ship serving in the Mediterranean. Built in 1922 by Cammell Laird & Company at Birkenhead in England, the 4,540-ton ship ran between Marseilles and the North African ports of Bone and Philippeville. 377 feet long, she had accommodations for 78 passengers in First Class, 150 in Tourist Class and up to 793 in what was called Fourth Class. During the War, in July 1942, she was seized by the Italians and used as the *Nicostra*. Italian Line served as her managers. A year later, she passed to the Germans, who employed her as the hospital ship *Giessen*. When the Allied armies invaded southern France in August 1944, she was deliberately scuttled at La Ciotat by the retreating Nazi forces. Later salvaged, she had to be thoroughly rebuilt before returning to CGT service. Broken up at La Spezia in Italy in the spring of 1963, she had reached the age of 41. *Eric Johnson Collection.*

Marigot This 4,087-ton 'fruit boat' was built in 1932 by Ateliers et Chantiers de St. Nazaire as the *Ardèche* for the Compagnie Générale d'Armements Maritimes. She ran in both North African and West Indies service. On the former route she carried large numbers of sheep. Transferred to CGT in 1939, she survived the War intact and then, for a time in the late 1940s and early 1950s, served on the Marseilles – North Africa passenger run. The 325-foot long ship went to the scrappers in 1954.
Eric Johnson Collection.

Ville d'Alger and Ville d'Oran

At just about the same time as the great *Normandie* was being completed, the Compagnie Générale Transatlantique was also creating what were then the two largest, fastest and probably finest passenger ships for Mediterranean service. The *Ville d'Alger* and *Ville d'Oran* were built at St. Nazaire and at La Ciotat in 1935 and 1936 respectively. Originally, each had two funnels but the second ones were removed during the War. Both ships assisted in the Norwegian campaign in the spring of 1940 and then, that June, carried Bank of France gold reserves to Casablanca and Dakar. The *Ville d'Alger* was later seized by the Germans, used as an accommodation ship for the military, then deliberately set on fire and finally scuttled as a blockship at Port du Bouc by their retreating forces in

August 1944. She was salvaged during the following winter. The *Ville d'Oran*, shown at Valletta on October 4th 1945, was used as an Allied trooper under Cunard-White Star management.
Richard Faber Collection and Michael Cassar Collection.

The 9,890-ton *Ville d'Alger* resumed her French Line sailings to North Africa in July 1948. With a speed of up to 21 knots, she mostly ran a service out of Marseilles to Bone and Philippeville. Other trips took her to Oran, Algiers, Mostaganem and Tunis.
Eric Johnson Collection.

As on her sistership, the accommodations on the *Ville d'Oran* were divided into three classes. Her exact configuration was 149 in First Class, 334 in Tourist Class and 671 in Fourth Class. Both ships had partial air-conditioning by the late 1950s but this was limited to the First Class public rooms.
Eric Johnson Collection.

In this aerial view, the *Ville d'Oran* is loading passengers at Tunis in 1955.
Cronican-Arroyo Collection.

After thirty years of service, both ships were retired by CGT in 1965-66. They were sold to Greek buyers, the Typaldos Lines, for Eastern Mediterranean passenger service. The *Ville d'Alger* was renamed *Poseidon* and the *Ville d'Oran* was called *Mount Olympos* (seen here). One of their fleetmates at the time was another ex-CGT ship, the former *Colombie*, which became the *Atlantica*. But after the Typaldos company collapsed, these ex-French ships were laid up. The former *Ville d'Alger* went to the breakers at La Spezia in April 1969, while the ex-*Ville d'Oran* followed her to the scrappers, but at Trieste, in the following December.

Alex Duncan Collection.

Commandant Quère

This 4,400-ton ship was a newbuild following the Second World War. She was ordered by the French government from the John I. Thornycroft yard at Southampton, especially for the Corsican run. She was named in honor of the master of the Fraissinet ship *Général Bonaparte* who had shown great gallantry when his vessel was torpedoed in 1943. The new ship was, in fact, launched for the Fraissinet company but by the time she was completed she had been assigned to the CGT. 363 feet long, she sailed from both Marseilles and Nice to such ports as Ajaccio, Bastia, Ile Rousse and Calvi. She was able to accommodate just under 1,000 passengers – 204 in First Class, 146 in Third and up to 644 in Fourth. Only two cabins, the First Class suites, had their own, private bathroom facilities. The ship remained in CGT service until broken up in 1968.

Eric Johnson Collection.

Cyrnos The *Cyrnos*, built in 1929 by the Germans, by A. G. Weser at Bremen, was notable for her Maierform bow. A 2,400-tonner, she was placed on the Compagnie Fraissinet's overnight run between Marseilles and Corsica. She had difficult times during the mid-1940s. Having been seized by the Nazis in 1943 and then scuttled by their retreating forces at Marseilles in August 1944, she was raised and repaired. But she sank at her moorings at La Ciotat during a gale in September 1947. However, she was a survivor and was again raised and restored. In May 1948, she was transferred to CGT and ran for them until broken up at La Seyne in 1968. She had accommodations for 151 passengers in First Class, 99 in Third and 350 in Fourth. *Eric Johnson Collection.*

Fred Scamaroni

This 1,900-ton ship – with quarters for just over 300 passengers (100 First Class, 30 Second and 204 Fourth) – joined the CGT schedules in 1948 as a temporary replacement for the company's war losses. She had been built at Fredrikstad back in 1923 as the *Kong Dag* for Det Sondenfjelds-Norske's service between Oslo and Kiel. She was bought by the French government in 1946 and was assigned to CGT two years later for their Corsican service. The 14-knot ship was placed in reserve for three years beginning in 1953, but then went to the breakers at La Spezia. *Eric Johnson Collection.*

Ville d'Ajaccio Here was another ship which had an adventurous war. A 2,444-tonner, she was built at Port du Bouc in 1929 and started her career in the Compagnie Fraissinet's Marseilles – Corsica service. She was torpedoed while sailing off St. Tropez in 1943 but managed to reach port and was saved. The 269-foot long vessel was transferred to CGT in 1948 and ran for them until as late as 1960. She was listed as having space for 140 passengers, divided between First and Second Class, and a further 120 in Fourth Class. She was sold to Far Eastern buyers who sailed her under the Panamanian flag and called her *East Wind*. But her new career was a very short one. A year later, in 1961, she went to Hong Kong scrappers.
Eric Johnson Collection.

On a westbound crossing in late August 1939, the 49,746-ton *Europa* of the North German Lloyd was about to head into the Atlantic on a voyage to New York when she was ordered by the Nazi High Command to return to her home port of Bremerhaven. Blacked out and maintaining radio silence, she reversed course and, on arrival, off-loaded her worried passengers back onto the dockside. A few days later, war began. The 936-foot long ship was soon repainted in gray and used as a permanently stationed accommodation centre for crews of the German Navy. During 1940, she sailed to Hamburg – just as her near-sister *Bremen* had done – and was to be converted for use in the intended sea invasion of Britain. Within a short time, however, the concept was abandoned and the former Atlantic speed champion (she had held the Blue Riband from 1930 until 1933) returned to Bremerhaven. She was nearby when, in March 1941, the *Bremen* was destroyed by fire, but the *Europa* remained unharmed. She thus became Germany's largest liner. In 1942, a rumor suggested that she would be rebuilt as an aircraft carrier.

When Allied invasion forces reached Bremerhaven in May 1945, the *Europa* was a sorry sight, neglected and rusting. Despite proposals to sink her toward the end of the War, she had remained afloat. She was put under the American flag and designated as the troopship *USS Europa*. She is seen here, at Bremerhaven, going into drydock for the first time in over five years. The date is June 20th 1945. *Cronican-Arroyo Collection.*

The Beautiful Liberté

Having been North German Lloyd's 936-foot *Europa*, completed in 1930 and for a time the fastest liner on the Atlantic, she sat out the War years virtually untouched, unharmed but sorely neglected. After Germany's defeat she was passed over, in 1945-46, to the Americans, then to the International Reparations Commission and finally to the French. Renamed *Liberté* (*Lorraine* had been the first choice), she was heiress to the grand legacy of the likes of the exceptional *Normandie*. It took nearly four years to bring her back to service, partly due to a shipyard fire in October 1949. The somewhat heavy Teutonic interiors of the 51,839-ton ship gave way to a lighter, almost late Art Deco, Gallic style. Evidently, the process was a huge success. The New York Herald Tribune wrote at the time, "The first thing that strikes you about this ship is her complete and utter Frenchiness."

Twice, she had nearly been lost. While fitting out as the *Europa* in March 1929, she caught fire at her shipyard berth in Hamburg and was so badly damaged as to be very nearly declared a total loss. Repairs and rebuilding added another year to her construction. Then, in December 1946, just after she had been handed over to the French, the still unrestored *Liberté* was ripped from her Le Havre moorings by a storm and, completely adrift, slammed into the sunken wreckage of the liner *Paris*, which had capsized after a fire back in April 1939. With her hull breached and seriously flooded, the ex-*Europa* might have been given up as a loss. But French Line engineers were optimistic. Patched, pumped out and refloated, the damaged ship was towed to the big St. Nazaire shipyards for a massive renewal.

After just a few transatlantic troop sailings for the Americans, the *Europa* gained the reputation of being a troubled ship. In particular, she was plagued by small fires. Furthermore, some serious cracks had been discovered in her hull. In early 1946, she was handed over to the International Reparations Commission. The French had the strongest claim to a large liner, having lost the *Normandie* in 1942. They were anxious to re-establish their luxurious pre-War service to New York. And so, it was thought, with proper modifications the German *Europa* could become the French *Liberté*. She finished her last US troop sailing in May 1946 and then went to Le Havre, where she was renamed in an official ceremony. *Cronican-Arroyo Collection.*

Restyled to carry as many as 1,502 passengers (555 in luxurious First Class, 497 in Cabin and 450 in economical Tourist), she crossed from New York to Plymouth or Southampton and then to Le Havre in 6 days. High summer season rates in the early 1950s were set at $330 in First Class, $210 in Cabin and $163 in Tourist. She was one of the largest, most popular and, typically for the French, best fed liners afloat.

Her interiors made a great impression on almost all who saw her. C. M. Squarey wrote, "The cavalcade of public rooms on the very wide, glass-enclosed Promenade Deck is really something to behold. Standing at the forward end in the Smoking Room and from there looking aft, the eye gazes upon a sight not seen in any other ship – an uninterrupted view some 495 feet long." Of the Grand Salon he wrote, "I have seen many rooms in many ships, but I think perhaps none has quite such an aristocratic look about it as this noble salon." The *Liberté* was capped by two enormous funnels and two extremely tall masts. Those funnels were heightened by domed, ventilator-fitted tops in the 1954 winter refit.

Very occasionally, the quadruple-screw liner dabbled in cruising: a trip to Rio for Carnival in 1953, a two-week Caribbean sailing in 1960. But it was clear that her days were numbered when, starting in 1957, construction began on the large, new flagship *France*, which was due to enter Atlantic service in 1962. There were rumors that the *Liberté* might go to Seattle for use as a floating hotel during the 1962 World's Fair, but this never came to pass. Following a tug and fireboat send-off at New York in November 1961, this grande dame returned to Le Havre for the last time and was decommissioned. Much of her furnishing went on the block and some of it found its way into the Sagamore Hotel in upstate New York. The old ship herself sailed around to La Spezia in Italy and a waiting team of demolition men.

Misfortune seemed to follow the *Liberté*. On December 8th 1946, she was pulled from her moorings at Le Havre by a strong Atlantic gale, slammed into the wreck of the liner *Paris* (on the left, sunk in 1938 and not yet salvaged due to the War), canted over for a time and then settled in the harbor. She had a large gash in her starboard side, but fortunately remained in an upright position. *Cronican-Arroyo Collection.*

The serious breach was at the level of the engine room. There was extensive flooding and so any thoughts of initial refit work gave way to salvage. She was not refloated for four months, until April 15th 1947.
Author's Collection.

The *Liberté* was towed to the Penhoët shipyard in the spring of 1947 and her $19 million restoration finally began. But then there were still more tense moments. In October 1949, a fire destroyed much of the new passenger accommodations. This delayed her return to service still further.
Cronican-Arroyo Collection.

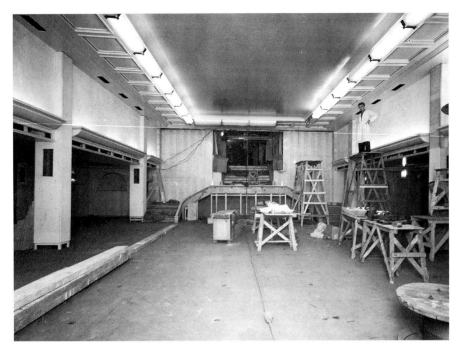

In triumph, the restyled, renewed *Liberté* arrived at New York for the first time as a French liner on the 23rd August 1950. She was the new flagship of the CGT (or Transat as it was sometimes known). She was immediately teamed with the celebrated *Ile de France* and so the proud French had two large luxury liners in North Atlantic service. In this dramatic aerial view, Cunard's *Caronia* is on the left and a small French Line freighter is on the south side of Pier 88. *Port Authority of New York & New Jersey.*

A few days later, following welcoming luncheons and dinners, tours and other celebrations, the *Liberté* made a late afternoon departure on her maiden eastbound crossing. It was purposely timed for a mid-Hudson River meeting with the inbound *Ile de France*.
Cronican-Arroyo Collection.

In the pre-dawn darkness of an October morning in 1953, the *Liberté* docks herself slowly and skilfully without the aid of Moran tugs, which were on strike. One of the liner's lifeboats has been lowered to act as a guide and for the transfer of some lines.
Cronican-Arroyo Collection.

"The fourth largest liner in the world, the *Liberté* has gained fame for her opulent settings, remarkable stability in all sorts of weather and the indefinable ambiance inherent in all French Line ships" was the claim made by her owners in a 1950s press release. Indeed, she was a ship of exceptional style. The Grand Salon, for example, located on the Promenade Deck and two decks high, was said to be a room "more likely found on land than aboard a ship!" *Cronican-Arroyo Collection.*

The stylish Winter Garden, which was located in the forward section of the superstructure. *Cronican-Arroyo Collection.*

The indoor pool aboard the *Liberté* was finished in glazed tiles and mosaics and was bordered by a small bar. It was located on F Deck.
Cronican-Arroyo Collection.

Hollywood afloat: the bedroom of the Provence Suite aboard the *Liberté*.
Cronican-Arroyo Collection.

The Cabin Class Main Lounge, located on the Promenade Deck, was a particularly light and spacious room thanks to the large bay windows. *Cronican-Arroyo Collection.*

The Cabin Class Smoking Room Bar, located on Main Deck, had an Art Deco style. *Cronican-Arroyo Collection.*

Some 60 per cent of the *Liberté*'s Cabin Class staterooms were outside, but this three-berth room was an exception. *Cronican-Arroyo Collection.*

During her 1954 winter refit at St. Nazaire, the *Liberté*'s original stacks were heightened with smoke-deflecting dome tops. She could now boast two of the mightiest funnels afloat, which somehow made the 51,839-ton liner seen even bigger in this wintry New York scene. *Cronican-Arroyo Collection.*

A rare occasion in 1957 when both the *Liberté* and the *Ile de France* were in New York at the same time. The Cunard freighter *Alsatia* is in the lower left position and beyond the *Ile* are two United States Lines ships, the freighter *American Flyer* and the liner *America*; and finally, the *Augustus* of the Italian Line.
Cronican-Arroyo Collection.

After a career of 31 years, the *Liberté* left New York in a gala farewell departure in November 1961. While there was some suggestion that she might be used as a floating hotel at Seattle for the 1962 World's Fair, the French Line was especially fearful of some "undignified" end coming to their former flagship. They recalled only too well what had happened to the beloved *Ile de France* at the hands of Hollywood film-makers in 1959. And so, the *Liberté* was sold to an intermediary, a Liechtenstein holding company, and then to Italian shipbreakers. She arrived at La Spezia on January 30th 1962 and, by June, was gone completely.
Moran Towing & Transportation Co.

Ville de Marseille / Maroc

She and her sister, the *Ville de Tunis*, were the first CGT newbuildings for the North African service after the Second World War. They came out in 1951-52 and, in some ways, their design was a preface to that of the larger, more elaborate *Antilles* and *Flandre*. Each of the African ships had a particularly sleek appearance, dominated by a Strombos-type funnel. Those funnels, intended to reduce the amount of smoke and smuts falling on deck, were not very successful in the end, however. The *Ville de Marseille* was also the first French passenger ship to  be fitted with stabilizers. Intended for the Marseilles – Algiers service, she was rerouted while still under construction, being reassigned to the Bordeaux – Casablanca run. This was a 53-hour passage in both directions. Her accommodations were arranged for 151 in First Class, 234 in Second, 143 in Third, 50 in Fourth and a further 200 on deck. At the end of her first Moroccan season, in December 1951, she was very suitably renamed *Maroc*. This lasted until 1956, when she was refitted and assigned to North African sailings. When the French Mediterranean services were regrouped and merged in 1969, she passed to the new Compagnie Générale Transméditerranée. But her days were numbered. New competitors arrived, in the form of big car ferries as well as nationalist tonnage belonging to the newly independent North African countries, and so she was sent to Bilbao in Spain for scrapping in the summer of 1973. *French Line.*

Ville de Tunis

This 9,226-ton sistership to the *Ville de Marseille* entered the Marseilles – North African service in March 1952. Her voyages varied to African ports: Oran, Algiers, Philippeville, Bone, Mostaganem and Tunis. She had accommodations for 149 passengers in First Class, 334 Tourist Class and 494 Fourth Class. She was partially air-

conditioned and all of her First Class cabins had private bathrooms. In 1967, she was sold to Kyriakos Lines of Greece and placed on the overnight run between Piraeus and Heraklion in Crete as the *Megalonissos Kriti*. Two years later, her name was changed to *City of Athens*. However, she spent many years in lay up in Perama Bay before leaving under tow for Barcelona on March 14th 1980. She was bound for the scrappers but, on the way, she encountered heavy weather and sank off the Balearic Islands on March 26th. *Eric Johnson Collection.*

Sampiero Corso

This 4,014-ton ship was built in 1936 for the French government's mail service to Corsica. She was managed by Fraissinet then. During the War, in 1942, she was seized by the Italians, who renamed her *Canosa*. In September 1943, she fell into German hands, only to be scuttled by them during their retreat the following year. Salvaged at Cassis in December 1945, she was towed to Toulon and left to await repairs. The 345-foot long ship was finally restored in 1949-51 for the CGT and resumed her place on the Corsica run out of Marseilles and Nice. She had accommodations for 113 in First Class, 115 Third and 596 Fourth. Finally, in 1967, she was sold to Far Eastern-Panamanian buyers, the Fortune Navigation Maritime Co., and became the *Fortune Mariner*. Her new life was brief, however, as she went to Hong Kong breakers in October 1968. *Eric Johnson Collection.*

Charles Plumier

When built as a "banana boat" for the Cie. Générale d'Armements Maritimes in 1938, she carried just 12 passengers. A 4,626-tonner, she was seized by the British during the War, became the ocean boarding vessel *H.M.S. Largs* and took part in the Sicily landings and the Normandy invasion, and in the landings in the South of France and at Rangoon. She was returned to the French in November 1945 and was reconditioned as a freighter.

Passing to the CGT in 1948, she was rebuilt to carry 77 passengers (14 First, 38 Tourist and 25 Fourth) on the Marseilles – North Africa run. She was also used in the Corsican service and, after 1960, on the Bordeaux – Casablanca run. Her French career ended in 1964, when she was sold to Greek buyers, the Kavounides Shipping Company, who renamed her *Pleias*. They were developing their cruise business at the time and intended to convert the *Pleias* for that purpose, but somehow this never quite came to pass. Instead, they operated her on Greek inter-island sailings as a regular passenger vessel. In 1966, she was laid up and two years later she was scrapped in Italy. *Claude Molteni de Villermont Collection.*

Flandre

The *Flandre* had troubles even at the start of her long and varied career. And then the worst trouble, a devastating fire, killed her off in the end. In the beginning, in July 1952, she broke down on her maiden voyage across the Atlantic. She finally reached New York harbor – only to break down again. She could not raise her anchors or blast her whistle. She had to be towed to her Manhattan pier for what had been planned as a news-making, celebratory arrival. She was, after all, one of her country's first brand new luxury liners since the crippling losses of the Second World War. To add to French embarrassment, this maiden voyage fiasco came only weeks after the stunning, record-breaking success of America's *United States*.

The 20,400-ton *Flandre* later changed hands, to Costa Line and finally to Epirotiki as the *Pallas Athena*. But fire, historically so often a problem for French-built passenger ships, finished her. On March 24th 1994, the 600-foot long ship burned in the harbor of Piraeus, Greece. Still smouldering, she was towed to open waters and declared a wreck.

The French Line had lost a good part of their splendid fleet in the War years, including the ultra-luxurious *Normandie*. But the celebrated *Ile de France* and the smaller *De Grasse* survived and then, through reparations, the line inherited Germany's giant *Europa*, which was promptly rechristened *Liberté*. But for brand new tonnage, the Parisian directors were more conservative, specifying medium-sized liners which included a pair of 800-passenger sisterships, the *Antilles* and the *Flandre*.

After extensive and expensive repairs to the faulty boilers and electrical gear which had turned her maiden voyage into a disaster, the 22-knot *Flandre* entered regular service on the North Atlantic, between Le Havre, Southampton and New York. At first partnering the *Ile de*

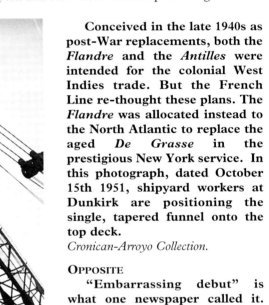

Conceived in the late 1940s as post-War replacements, both the *Flandre* and the *Antilles* were intended for the colonial West Indies trade. But the French Line re-thought these plans. The *Flandre* was allocated instead to the North Atlantic to replace the aged *De Grasse* in the prestigious New York service. In this photograph, dated October 15th 1951, shipyard workers at Dunkirk are positioning the single, tapered funnel onto the top deck.
Cronican-Arroyo Collection.

OPPOSITE

"Embarrassing debut" is what one newspaper called it. Led by the nose by Moran tugs, the *Flandre* limped into New York harbor on July 30 1952, concluding a maiden voyage that was marred by mechanical mishaps. Even within the confines of the Lower Bay, the ship was forced to remain off Staten Island for as long as 6 hours before sufficient power could be mustered even to raise her anchors. Then, with only one screw turning, she was towed by four tugs to Pier 88. She was 23 hours late. It was a bitter pill for the French Line to swallow for she had been billed as the newest and finest post-War French passenger ship.
Cronican-Arroyo Collection.

France and the *Liberté*, she later sailed with the sumptuous new *France* in 1962. She was then transferred to join her sister, *Antilles*, in the Caribbean service. There were also some air-sea cruises out of Martinique which were marketed to North American travellers. In 1968, she was sold to Italy's Costa Line. Rebuilt as a cruise ship and renamed *Carla C.*, she went directly on charter to Princess Cruises and sailed from West Coast ports as their *Princess Carla*. But Costa soon recalled the ship for their own Lower Caribbean service out of San Juan, in which she enjoyed great success. She was given major surgery at Amsterdam in 1974, when her steam turbines were replaced by new Dutch diesels. Later called *Carla Costa*, she was finally sold to Epirotiki in 1992.

Running mostly 7-day cruises to the Aegean islands and Turkey as the *Pallas Athena*, she collided with Windstar's *Wind Spirit* in June 1993. When we saw her at Kusadasi two months later, she still had a nasty gash in her otherwise elegant, flared bow. The fire that destroyed her in 1994 started in a passenger cabin and then spread quickly. Her passengers had just disembarked and she was to sail again that same day.

The *Pallas Athena*'s demise was yet another act in something of a modern Greek tragedy that befell her Epirotiki owners. In 1988, their *Jupiter* sank outside Piraeus after a collision with an Italian freighter. In June 1991, the *Pegasus* burned out while docked at Venice and then, just two months later, the *Oceanos* made headline news when she sank in a gale off South Africa.

The 600-foot long *Flandre* was one of the most handsome liners of the 1950s. As built, the 20,477-ton ship could carry 402 passengers in First Class, 389 in Cabin Class and then a mere 97 in Tourist class.
Moran Towing & Transportation Co.

After her initial misfortunes, the *Flandre* became a popular ship. Here we see a portion of her First Class Restaurant. *Cronican-Arroyo Collection.*

Like other noted French Line ships, the *Flandre* had some splendid suites and cabins de luxe in First Class. Here is the bedroom of the Dunkerque Suite. *Richard Faber Collection.*

Another First Class suite, with its adjoining sitting room, on the *Flandre*.
Robert Pelletier Collection.

1950s French elegance on the *Flandre*. *Robert Pelletier Collection.*

The Cabin Class Salon and then the Cabin Class Restaurant aboard the *Flandre*. *Robert Pelletier Collection.*

Sold to Italy's Costa Line in early 1968, the former *Flandre* was extensively refitted as the cruiseship *Carla C.* Her accommodations were recreated for 754 all-First Class berths and, in addition, her exterior appearance was changed by a heightened funnel. *Costa Line.*

Bought by Greece's Epirotiki Lines in 1992 and renamed *Pallas Athena*, the ship is seen docked at Valletta in Malta. *Michael Cassar.*

Antilles – the "Aunt Tilly"

Passengers, crew, travel agents, but especially dockers – those infamous stevedores – have often dubbed ships with their own nicknames. The old Cunard *Mauretania* was "the Maury", for instance, and her running-mate, the *Berengaria*, was "the Berry". The *Majestic* was called the "Magic Stick" and, more recently, because of her less than easy working conditions, the *Southern Cross* was known to many among her crew as the "Suffering Cross". For other ships, it was purely a matter of language, of correct pronunciation. An example, the French Line's *Antilles* was known to English dockers and handlers, at Southampton and at Plymouth where she called regularly, as the "Aunt Tilly". She was also one of France's most popular post-Second World War liners.

As we have already seen, the French Line had a very depleted fleet after the War. Only three noted liners remained by 1945-46: the *Ile de France*, the sunken but salvaged *De Grasse* and the *Colombie*. And so, besides the rehabilitation and modernization of these ships and the rebuilding of the main terminal at Le Havre (in 1947-48), the company set in train the design of a pair of moderately sized 20,000-tonners. Having been given Germany's pre-War *Europa* which would join the North Atlantic service, CGT intended their two new ships for the colonial Caribbean run to Martinique, Guadeloupe and other ports. They would supplement the smaller 13,000-ton *Colombie*, which, after being rebuilt in 1948-50, was operating single-handedly. But by the early 1950s, there was an upswing in traffic on the North Atlantic. Furthermore, competitor companies were bringing out new ships of their own. Consequently, it was decided that

This photograph, taken at San Juan on June 17th 1955, shows the *Antilles* departing for Europe. Poetically photographed from within the El Morro Fortress, the sailing marked the beginning of French Line service to and from the Puerto Rican port as part of their regular Caribbean passenger schedule.
Cronican-Arroyo Collection.

61

Because of exhaust problems, the funnel aboard the *Antilles* was raised in height in the late 1950s and thereafter made her more distinguishable from the otherwise very similar *Flandre*. *Eric W. Johnson Collection.*

one of these new ships, the *Flandre*, would spend about 9 – 10 months every year in the New York service beginning in the summer of 1952. Her near-sister, the *Antilles*, followed in May 1953 but, as originally intended, was used exclusively for tropical duties.

"Smart looking" was the way one journalist described the pair. They had flared bows; single, tapered, rather squat stacks (later heightened on the *Antilles*); a lone mast above the wheelhouse and an even shorter one just aft of the funnel; and electric cranes in place of the traditional booms and kingposts. Sometimes known as "the white lady", the sleek *Antilles* made an especially striking sight in the tropic, blue waters of the Caribbean. At 599 feet in overall length, she was powered by steam turbines which produced a service speed of 22 knots.

Her 778 maximum passenger capacity was divided into three classes – 404 First Class, 285 Cabin Class and 89 Tourist Class. Her interiors were French contemporary. The First Class Main Lounge, for example, boasted heavily embroidered chairs quite similar to ones to be found on the exquisite *Normandie* in the mid-'thirties. A veranda "garden" lined each side of the lounge, complete with vibrant greenery and panels giving the impression of terra cotta bricks. The dance floor in the Smoking Room could be lit from below by dozens of multi-colored lights. Aft was the outdoor pool, which was illuminated in the evenings. There were also a good-sized gym, a gift shop

and a hair salon. The main Dining Room below could seat 214 at one sitting and was air-conditioned. All of the First Class staterooms, too, were air-conditioned and had at least a shower and toilet, but often a tub bath as well. The Cabin Class spaces, in keeping with a post-War trend amongst brand new liners, were almost of First Class standard.

Generally, the *Antilles* was routed from Le Havre and Southampton to Vigo (in northern Spain) and then to San Juan, Ponte à Pitre, Fort de France, La Guaira, Trinidad and Barbados. Homebound, in reverse, she did not call at La Guaira but put in at Plymouth instead of Southampton. The roundtrip took four weeks. There were also occasional Caribbean cruises. In the late 1960s, weekly 7-day cruises out of Fort de France were sold to North Americans, who used connecting flights on Air France from New York and from Miami. The *Flandre* joined her sister fulltime in 1962 but was sold off to the Costa Line in 1968. Thereafter, the *Antilles* sailed on alone. How much longer she might have survived is in some question. Her career ended abruptly when she caught fire on January 8 1971 off the island of Mustique. She burned out and had to be abandoned. Her 635 passengers and crew were rescued by the *Queen Elizabeth 2* and two nearby French Line freighters. Left on a reef, the blackened corpse of the *Antilles* broke in three and gradually fell into the sea.

Comfort onboard the *Antilles*: the elegant First Class Main Lounge and Le Palm Beach, the ship's lido area. In the latter view, the speeding *Ile de France* can be seen in the background. *Richard Faber Collection.*

Ville de Bordeaux

Although launched in 1940, this ship was not completed until 1946, having been delayed by the War. Named the *Saga*, she was built in Sweden for Svenska Lloyd. She entered service between Gothenburg and London in May 1946 and was an earlier, motor-driven version of the *Patricia* of 1951, which went on to become the cruise ship *Ariadne*. Despite being noted for their fine accommodation and splendid cuisine, the two ships were adversely affected by air competition and *Saga* was sold to CGT in 1956. Renamed *Ville de Bordeaux* and rated at 6,541 gross tons, she was placed in the Bordeaux – Casablanca service and later, after 1960, ran between Marseilles and Corsica. Partially air-conditioned, her accommodations were listed as 181 in First Class, 144 Tourist and 66 Fourth Class (this was later amended to 130 First and 300 Tourist). She was sold to the Bulgarian government shipping company in 1964 and was renamed *Nessebar* for service between Varna and Istanbul, as well as some Mediterranean cruising. She arrived at Split on Christmas Day 1975 for breaking up. *Richard Faber Collection.*

The Splendid France

The *France* was the most luxurious superliner of her time. She was big (over 66,000 gross tons), very fast (30 knots was her average speed) and the flagship of the entire French merchant marine. Charles de Gaulle took a very personal interest in her construction, from 1957 until her maiden voyage in early 1962. Costing no less than $80 million, she was made of the very best materials by the very best artisans. Even though the jets had already arrived on the transatlantic scene (in October 1958), the 1,035 feet-long *France* (for many years the longest liner in the World) steamed into New York harbor to a gala welcome: dozens of tugs, spraying fireboats, planes and helicopters overhead. Her future seemed assured.

British puppeteer John Chisholm had heard of the splendid *France*, but never dreamed of sailing aboard her, particularly on what was perhaps her most glamorous voyage – her first three-month trip around the World, a highly publicized, expensive sailing which began in January 1972. "I was performing on a westbound crossing of the *QE2* in November 1971 when I met a man from the French Line who was going to New York to prepare all the docking arrangements for the *France*'s 30-port world voyage. It seems he enjoyed my puppet show and he hired me for the *France*'s world cruise."

Newspapers and magazines ran special articles about the lavish trip, the first world cruise in French Line history. The *France* was already acclaimed as "the finest French restaurant anywhere in the World", her wine cellars were the largest afloat and her normal capacity of just over 2,000 was purposely reduced to under 1,200 for this trip. It was said that the entire sailing took two years to plan and organize. Extra linens had to be flown out to the ship, for example, and refuelling tankers planned several rendez-vous stops. Some of the best European performers were flown out at sequenced intervals to join the cruise.

"The magic of the trip started from the very beginning. On the flight from Paris out to Hong Kong, where I was to join the *France*, I was presented with a bottle of Moët & Chandon. It was sent by the French Line," recalled John Chisholm. "I did two shows on the segment between Hong Kong and Cape Town. One of the other acts, a magician, travelled with his own leopard."

"The *France* was really a great backdrop, a grand setting if you will, for the passengers. She was really very functional, almost utilitarian in her décor," added Chisholm. "She was like a great stage set. There were lots of nylon fabrics and foam-backed chairs and muted colors, all of which made the passengers themselves stand out, even shine. There was none of today's overwhelming opulence."

"The passengers were all rich and very well travelled. There were lots of French, other Europeans and not only North Americans but South Americans as well. I met many of them at the elaborate midnight buffets. There were also many theme nights onboard. Sailing out of Bombay, for example, there was 'A Night of the Maharajas'. The ladies were all exquisitely dressed in newly bought saris, but the men were quite amazing as well. Many had costumes made onshore with those high Indian collars and topped by jewelled turbans. After Colombo, we had 'Sapphire Night'. Everyone wore sapphires and sometimes dressed in sapphire blue costumes. Otherwise, there were ladies who wore full white mink stoles. One exception, however, was a little Frenchman who wore the same suit every single day!"

"Of course, the food and the service were magnificent," concluded John Chisholm. "No ship had better kitchens then. She deserved her reputation right down to the last dessert."

The *France* made a second world cruise in the winter of 1974, but was retired and laid up later that same year. She had become uneconomic, especially to her benefactors, the French government. In 1979, she was sold to Norwegian Caribbean Lines, who rebuilt her as the tropical cruise ship *Norway*. She still plies the Caribbean out of Miami, but she made a nostalgic crossing to Le Havre, her onetime homeport, in September 1996 and then returned to European waters briefly in 1998.

An artist's rendering of the forthcoming new superliner *France*, first released in 1957, showing her with two conventional funnels. *Cronican-Arroyo Collection.*

OPPOSITE PAGE
Prefabricated construction systems, advanced for their time, were used in the building of the *France*. After the first keel plates were laid on October 7th 1957, huge sections – some weighing as much as 50 tons – were assembled at St. Nazaire.
Cronican-Arroyo Collection.

RIGHT

The 1,035-foot long *France* took 4 years, 3 months and 28 days to build. Her creation was considered a national morale-builder following the tragedies of colonial Algeria.
Richard Faber Collection.

BELOW

Initial studies suggested that one 66,000-ton liner would be far superior, at least in North Atlantic express service, to two more conventional 30,000-tonners; and that a two-class ship would be more suitable for current requirements than a traditional three-class vessel.
Cronican-Arroyo Collection.

The *France* had a unique 'double bottom' incorporating an inner keel with storage space for enough fuel and water for a two-way crossing of the Atlantic without refuelling.
Cronican-Arroyo Collection.

The *France* just before her ceremonial launching on May 11th 1960. *Richard Faber Collection.*

Madame de Gaulle was godmother to the *France* at the naming and launch ceremony in May 1960. The General himself gave a stirring speech on the triumphs of the liner's creation and on the special bond linking the French and American peoples. *Cronican-Arroyo Collection.*

To great cheers, the *France* slips into the waters at St. Nazaire. *Richard Faber Collection.*

Now afloat, the *France* awaits the invasion of some 2,000 workers who will complete the fitting out and apply the finishing touches. The work took eighteen months. *Richard Faber Collection.*

The two giant funnels, built ashore and fitted aboard in the spring of 1961, were of the most radical design. They were crowned by pairs of ailerons, which served as exhausts. This big wing design gave a streamlined, very modernistic look to the ship while lifting smoke up and away from her decks. *Richard Faber Collection.*

Each funnel also had an elaborate filtering device which removed solids from the smoke and then returned them to the bowels of the ship.
Fred Rodriguez Collection.

The ship's funnels became her instantly recognisable trademark. A model of one was sent on tour round France. It was used as a promotional office.
Cronican-Arroyo Collection.

The four massive propellers – each weighing 27 tons and measuring 18 feet in diameter – had gone aboard in July 1961. Four months later, the *France* was ready for sea trials. With only the slightest vibrations, she reached 34.13 knots, using nine-tenths of her full power (146,000 horsepower against a potential 160,000). *Richard Faber Collection.*

On January 19th 1962, the *France* left Le Havre on a 'shake down' cruise to the Canary Islands – filled to capacity and proving herself beyond reproach. *Richard Faber Collection.*

The *France* intrigued the travelling public and dazzled the press. When she first reached New York on February 8th 1962, she was given an immensely enthusiastic reception. *Cronican-Arroyo Collection.*

A classic gathering along New York's 'Luxury Liner Row' on a busy summer's day, July 10th 1963. Six liners are in port together – from top to bottom, they are the *Independence*, *Leonardo da Vinci*, *Atlantic*, *Olympia*, *France* and *Queen Mary*. At the far right is the Danish freighter *Benny Skou*, then on charter to Cunard. *Flying Camera, Inc.*

The *France*'s modern interiors included a splendid range of suites and cabins de luxe on the upper decks. Some of the larger ones included private dining rooms with adjoining areas where food could be kept warm.
Frank O. Braynard Collection.

There were no traditional wood finishes on the *France*. The décor featured aluminium, formica and even industrial plastic. This view shows the Grand Salon Fontainebleau.
Frank O. Braynard Collection.

In the waning days of the old trans-Atlantic liner trade, three of the final superliners are together on a gloomy winter's afternoon, February 3rd 1973. The *Michelangelo* is on the left, the *Queen Elizabeth 2* in the center and the *France* on the right.
Flying Camera Inc.

End of an era: members of the ship's hotel staff meet on the quayside at Le Havre to demonstrate against plans to decommission the giant *France* in October 1974. They delayed her departure for New York. *Richard Faber Collection.*

The *France* was idle in a backwater at Le Havre for nearly five years. Her great lounges were silent and lonely, some of the furnishings overlaid with dust-covers. *Hapag-Lloyd Shipyard.*

The First Class Chambord Dining Room, one of the most exquisite rooms ever to put to sea, was used for a collection of odd chairs during the ship's 'silent period'. *Hapag-Lloyd Shipyard.*

After being sold for $18 million to the Norwegian Caribbean Lines for conversion to the tropical cruise ship *Norway*, the *France* was towed from Le Havre on August 22nd 1979. She was taken to the Hapag-Lloyd yard at Bremerhaven. Her conversion would cost her new owners $80 million.
Hapag-Lloyd Shipyard.

Now flying the Norwegian colors, the former *France* is seen at Bremerhaven on August 25th 1979. The key to her subsequent conversion and operation was economy. Only one engine room would be used, for example, since she would now have a fuel-saving service speed of 16 knots (against the 30 knots of her French Line days). The staff would be reduced from its extravagant French level of 1,100 to 800, while the overall passenger capacity would be increased from 2,044 to 2,181. *Hapag-Lloyd Shipyard.*

Since entering Miami-Caribbean service in May 1980, the *Norway* has returned to Germany on several occasions for further refit and repair work. In this view, at Bremerhaven on July 3rd 1982, she is entering one of that port's locks stern first. *Steffen Weirauch.*

Greatly refitted and with the addition of two upper decks, the *Norway* of the now renamed Norwegian Cruise Lines arrives in familiar waters: New York's Hudson River. The date is August 1997. *Richard Faber Collection.*

De Grasse (1956)

When the French Line lost their Caribbean liner *Antilles* in January 1971, they were desperate to find a replacement. Quickly, they bought the Norwegian America Line's *Bergensfjord*, built in 1956 for service on the North Atlantic and for cruising. She was delivered to the French in the fall of 1971. They renamed her *De Grasse* (*Louisianne* had been the original choice) and refitted her to carry 580 all-First Class passengers. Although she was used for some Caribbean sailings from Le Havre, her mainstay was cruising. But after the dramatic international oil price increases in 1973, she was back on the sales lists. *French Line.*

Ironically, the 578-foot long *De Grasse* was resold to the Norwegians, to Thoresen & Co., who placed her under Singapore registry as the *Rasa Sayang*. She ran two-week cruises between Singapore and Indonesia. The programme was interrupted by a serious fire in 1977 and, although she was repaired and returned to service, she never regained her old following and was soon laid-up and offered for sale. In 1978, she went to Cypriot-flag Greek owners who renamed her *Golden Moon*. She was rumored to become the Dutch-chartered

Prins Van Oranje and, when that failed to materialize, she was chartered to CTC Lines, once again as the *Rasa Sayang*. She was, in fact, undergoing an extensive overhaul and refit at Perama in Greece when, on August 27th 1980, she was swept by fire. She was towed into the shallow reaches of the harbor and then allowed to capsize. Her remains lie quite close to those of another fire-gutted cruiseship, the restyled *Reina del Mar*, which had once been the *Ocean Monarch* of the Furness-Bermuda Line. *Gerhard Fiebiger.*

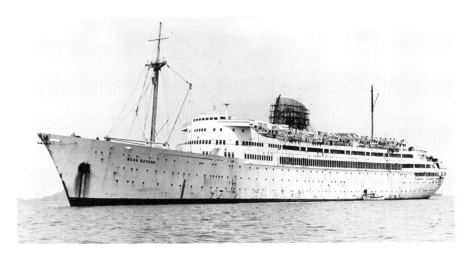

Napoléon This 5,802-ton passenger-car ferry began a new generation of ships on CGT's Mediterranean routes. Launched at La Seyne in April 1959, she entered service in the following January. Quite advanced for her time, she had a bow propeller to ease manoeuvring in confined areas; garage space for up to 100 cars which were driven onboard through side-doors; 3 holds, including cold chambers; cafeteria dining; and interchangeable cabin accommodations. Her service speed varied according to demand: using four engines, she could do 18 knots; on just two engines she could manage 14 $1/2$ knots. Partially air-conditioned, her accommodations on the Corsican run were arranged as 165 First, 30 interchangeable between First and Second, 276 Second and 753 Fourth class. She had fourteen years with CGT, being sold to Saudi Lines of Jeddah in 1974. She sailed as the pilgrim ship *Alpasha* until she was broken up in 1988. *French Line.*

Fred Scamaroni Built at La Seyne in 1966, this 4,771-ton car ferry differed from the successful *Napoléon* in a number of ways, particularly in that entrance to her car-deck was by way of bow and stern doors. She too was used in the Corsican service and she had space for up to 1,420 passengers in four classes, including 394 in First Class cabins. She was passed over to the new Cie. Générale Transméditerranéene in 1969 when CGT's Mediterranean services were combined with those of the Cie. Mixte; and then in 1976 she went to SNCM (Société Nationale Maritime Corse Méditerranée). But she was deemed too small and by 1980 she was sold to the Danish shipowner Ole Lauritzen for a new cross-Channel ferry service between Ramsgate and Dunkirk.

She was renamed *Nuits Saint Georges* but was arrested for debt later that same year, in November, and then laid up at Flushing. She went to Egyptian owners in 1982, becoming the *Lord Sinai*, then the *Al Tahra* and finally the *Salem Express*. Sadly, while on a Jeddah – Port Suez voyage in December 1991, she struck a reef during a storm and sank. Only 180 of the 664 onboard were saved. In this photograph, the *Fred Scamaroni* is seen at Marseilles on 14 May 1967. *V. H. Young and L. A. Sawyer.*

Corse

The 4,555-ton *Corse* was rather similar to the *Fred Scamaroni* and was built at St. Nazaire in 1966, also for the Corsican service. Certified to carry up to 1,408 passengers, she had provision for 96 cars. She too was transferred to the Cie. Générale Transméditerranéene in 1969 and then to SNCM in 1976. She was sold to Greek buyers in 1981 and was renamed *Golden Vergina*. She remained in service until the late 1990s. *Arnold Kludas Collection.*

Comte de Nice

A twin sister to the *Corse*, she was, however, built at Port du Bouc. Originally intended to be the *Provence*, she was completed as the *Comte de Nice*. Used on the Corsican run, she also passed to the Compagnie Générale Transméditerranéene in 1969 and then to SNCM in 1976. Like her sister, she was sold to Greek buyers, in 1983, and remains in service as the *Naias II*. *Alex Duncan.*

Rousillon

This 7,659-ton ferry was built by Wärtsilä at their yard at Abo in Finland in 1966. She was completed as the *Prins Hamlet* for Swedish owners, Lion Ferry AB. Later transferred to the West German flag and becoming

Prinz Hamlet, she traded mostly on the Bremerhaven – Harwich run. Certified to carry up to 1,200 passengers (including 200 in cabins and 750 in reclining chairs), this 440-footer was sold to CGT in 1970. It was intended that she be called *Languedoc*, but in the end she was named *Rousillon* instead and was transferred to Cie. Générale Transméditerranéene for Corsican service. In 1976, she went over to SNCM. She was displaced by newer, larger tonnage by 1980 and was sold to Greek buyers who called her *Kamiros*. She remains in Aegean service. *Gerhard Fiebiger.*

2
Compagnie des Messageries Maritimes

Messageries Maritimes has surely been France's second most important passenger ship company, being surpassed only by the CGT, the French Line. Messageries' roots are much earlier, dating from 1835 when, as a department of the French government, the Administration des Postes, they started a ten-steamer service between Marseilles and the Levant. In 1851, the service was transferred to another Government division, Messageries Nationales, which had charge of French road communications and transport. ("Messageries" means carriers or messengers.) By 1871, after several further name changes and with the company's interests expanded well east of Suez to the Far East, and also to Africa and South America, there was another change of name, to Compagnie des Messageries Maritimes, "MM" for short. As Duncan Haws wrote in his company fleet history, "Messageries Maritimes was henceforth the French state's chosen carrier for the Indian Ocean and Asiatic seaboards, and for the islands of the Pacific from Japan down to New Zealand."

By 1900, the company had 60 ships on almost worldwide services. MM continued to run French government and colonial service until the early 1970s, when, following the independence of most overseas colonies, the passenger fleet was phased out and government operating subsidies were cut by as much as 75%. In 1977, Messageries Maritimes was merged with CGT and together they were restyled as the CGM, Compagnie Générale Maritime. In due course, all remaining MM ships were phased out, with only some earlier company names being used as a reminder of the past. By the late 1990s, CGM itself was privatized by the French government, but conntainerships, some with 6 – 12 passenger berths, still ply many of the early MM routes. One service, sailing in 2000 between Marseilles and the Far East, is marketed as the French Asia Line.

Champollion

This three-funnel, 12,200-tonner was completed at La Ciotat in 1924. Used on the Marseilles – Alexandria service, she was rebuilt nine years later, in 1933, with a new, rounded Maierform bow and with additional turbines. As a result, her service speed increased from 17 to 19 knots and her overall length from 520 to 550 feet. Used by the Allies as a troopship during the War, she was not restored for commercial passenger service until 1950. Yet again, her appearance was changed

– she emerged with only a single, tapered stack. With berthing arrangements now of 207 passengers in First Class, 142 in Second and 150 in Third, she resumed Marseilles – Eastern Mediterranean sailings in March

1951. Her new career was brief, however. She was wrecked while approaching Beirut in bad weather on December 22nd 1952. Stranded on a reef only two miles south of the harbor entrance, *Champollion* lay just 200 yards from a nearby beach. But because of the heavy seas, her lifeboats could not be lowered. She began to list seriously and then cracked in two just aft of the funnel. However, through the extraordinary efforts of Beirut pilots and their crews, all but 15 onboard the stricken liner were rescued. The wreck of the *Champollion* was later sold to local Lebanese scrappers.

Hisashi Noma Collection and Alex Duncan.

Athos II By the late 1950s, the 15,275-ton passenger ship *Athos II* was the oldest member of the Messageries Maritimes fleet. She had been built in Germany, by AG Weser at Bremen, and completed in January 1927. Used on the long run from Marseilles to the Far East via the Suez Canal, she was extensively rebuilt in 1937-38. Her engines were upgraded and her passenger configuration was adjusted to 84 in First Class, 108 in Second and 112 in Third. Upon the fall of France in the spring of 1940, she was laid up at Algiers. *Richard Faber Collection.*

Seen here while docked at Brooklyn, New York on November 27th 1943, the *Athos II* had been taken over by the Allies in December 1942. Under the control of the War Shipping Administration in the United States, she sailed to ports throughout the World: Cape Town, Bora Bora, Rio de Janeiro, Fremantle, Bombay, Naples. At war's end in 1945, she made several New York – Southampton – Le Havre sailings before being returned to Messageries Maritimes in January 1946. Following a refit, she resumed Marseilles – Far East passenger service until being retired in 1959. That summer, she was delivered to breakers at La Spezia in Italy. *Frank O. Braynard Collection.*

Eridan

The 9,927-ton *Eridan* was built in 1928 at La Ciotat for the Marseilles – Far East service. Used as a trooper during and immediately after the Second World War, she was badly damaged by a fire at Saigon on December 29th 1945. She was later rebuilt thoroughly, with her two unusual square funnels being replaced by one more conventional stack. Her pre-War capacity of 570 was greatly reduced to 84 in First Class and 100 in Second Class. She resumed sailings on the Far East run in September 1951 but was sold to French shipbreakers at La Seyne in March 1956. *Hisashi Noma Collection and Alex Duncan.*

The *Félix Roussel* as built, with a black hull and her eccentric square funnels. *Arnold Kludas Collection.*

The 'White Swan' – Félix Roussel

Messageries Maritimes caused astonishment in the late 1920s by introducing a series of liners with square stacks – low and with a broad rim round the top. One of these unusual-looking ships was the *Félix Roussel*, a 16,700-tonner named for a former president of the line. She was launched at St. Nazaire in December 1929 by Ateliers et Chantiers de la Loire.

Completed in the fall of 1930, the 568-foot long liner joined the service linking the motherland of France with her colonies in Indo-China and with other Far Eastern ports – what the French called the Extreme Orient. From Marseilles she sailed via the Suez Canal to Djibouti, Colombo, Singapore, Saigon, Hong Kong,

Shanghai and Kobe, sometimes with stopovers at other ports. She was partnered by other Messageries Maritimes stalwarts such as 'The Three Musketeers' (*Athos II*, *Porthos* and *Aramis*), and *Président Doumer*. In the late 1930s, a first class ticket from Marseilles to Saigon cost from $420, while in third class the fare was from $190. The voyage took 23 days.

The *Félix Roussel* was, of course, a mailship and also carried lots of freight. She had accommodations for 398

The same ship took on a far more pleasing look following her 1948-50 rebuilding. *Marius Bar.*

86

During her Arosa Line period as the *Arosa Sun*, the former *Félix Roussel* sailed with both a black and a white hull. *FotoFlite.*

passengers – 196 in First Class, 113 in Second and 89 in Third. In First Class there were the high colonial officials and rich traders. Lower down the social scale were tourists, less senior civil servants, soldiers, police, artisans and migrants. Young Indo-Chinese used her to travel to school in Mother France.

Soon after the fall of France in 1940, while at Port Said, the *Félix Roussel* was seized by the Allies, who used her as a troopship. She was returned to her owners in 1947 and was given a very lengthy refit at Dunkirk. It was 1950 before she returned to service. Her appearance had been transformed by the removal of those strange square funnels and the substitution of a single, broad, raked but normally-shaped one. In the company's literature she was now sometimes referred to as a 'white swan' and, indeed, she was now a rather elegant-looking ship.

Internally, she was much as before. Décor in first class took its style from the Khmer period. The company issued a special book to remind the travelling public of her unique 'Oriental magnificence'. She really was magnificent (some might say, overwhelming), with an abundance of intricate carving. For instance, the first class dining room was, as usual on a French ship, entered down a broad staircase. The balustrades were splendidly carved and culminated at the bottom in two figures, each with seven heads spread out like a fan. The central section of the room suggested one of the open courtyards of Angkorvat, an impression accentuated by the carefully lit, blue ceiling which looked like the open sky. Other rooms were equally sumptuous. As one commentator wrote, 'She blends the French way of living with the splendours of an Oriental setting'.

But the troubles which preceded the granting of independence to the French colonies in Indo-China had a bad effect on the Messageries Maritimes service to the Extreme Orient. In 1955, the *Félix Roussel* was sold to the Arosa Line, a Swiss-based company who specialised in the emigrant trades and had grown at a great pace. They called their latest purchase *Arosa Sun* and registered her in Panama. They had her refitted to carry just 60 passengers in First Class, but nearly 900 in Tourist. Mainly, she sailed between Northern Europe and Canada but she also did some cruising from New York. In December 1958, Arosa collapsed. The *Arosa Sun* was at Bremerhaven, where she was impounded, eventually passing into the hands of a Swiss bank. In the end, she was sold to a firm of Dutch steelmakers who used her as a stationary accommodation ship for some of their workers. She lay at Ijmuiden until 1974. In that year, she was towed to Spain for scrapping.

Docked at Ijmuiden in Holland, the *Arosa Sun* served as a workers' accommodation ship for 14 years. *Luís Miguel Correia.*

Maréchal Joffre

Another pre-War Messageries Maritimes passenger ship which sailed throughout the 1950s was the 11,680-ton *Maréchal Joffre*. Built at La Ciotat in 1933, she was used in both the Marseilles – East Africa and Marseilles – Far East services. She was seized by the United States just after the attack on Pearl Harbor, in December 1941, and was later outfitted as the troop transport *USS Rochambeau*. She was returned to the French in the spring of 1945 and reverted to her original name. She underwent an extensive rebuilding in 1950, when her original twin squat funnels were replaced by a single larger one. Her accommodations were then set as 129 in First Class and 130 in Second Class. The *Maréchal Joffre* continued on the Far East run until 1959 and was delivered to Japanese scrappers at Osaka on January 15th 1960. In the second photograph, taken at Marseilles and showing an impressive array of Messageries Maritimes tonnage, the *Maréchal Joffre* is in the foreground with the *Felix Roussel*, the *Laos* and finally the *Viet-Nam* lying astern of her.

Alex Duncan and Richard Faber Collection.

Sagittaire

This 8,254-ton combination passenger-cargo ship reopened Messageries Maritimes' Marseilles – Panama – South Pacific service in March 1948. She had been fitted with accommodations for 37 First Class, 45 Second Class and 38 Third Class passengers as well as temporary berths for as many as 922 troops. She had been built for the French Line in 1929 by Bremer Vulkan at Vegesack in Germany. She was called *Washington* at that stage and was used in the Northern Europe – West Coast of North America service. She was transferred to Messageries Maritimes and renamed in 1938. The *Sagittaire* continued in Pacific passenger service, save for the War years, until early 1954, when her passenger quarters were removed. Soon afterward, she was sold to Hong Kong buyers using the Panamanian flag and became the *Pacific Glory*. Later, in 1956, she went to other Panamanian owners and was renamed *Oceanic Reliance*. She was sold to Japanese breakers in 1959 and was delivered at Mihara on October 10th. *Hisashi Noma Collection.*

La Marseillaise

When the luxury liner *La Marseillaise* started her maiden voyage on August 18th 1949, she was an early symbol of France's gradual recovery from the Second World War. She was the first big liner to be completed in a French yard since the end of hostilities. Designed for the vital colonial service between Marseilles and Indo-China, she had originally been laid down at the Chantiers Navals at La Ciotat in June 1939, with completion planned for 1943. Her construction went slowly during the first months of the War, and then stopped completely in June 1940, after the invasion of France. By then, only 200 tons of steel had been laid and it was not until the following December that construction was resumed. La Ciotat was then in the unoccupied area of France and the Vichy government wanted the various industries of this zone to have as much work as possible for French interests. It was at this time that the vessel, which had hitherto been known simply as *Numéro 161*, was given the name *Maréchal Pétain*. She was finally launched on June 10th 1944.

After the French liberation, the country's largely devastated shipbuilding industry had more urgent matters to deal with than completing luxury liners, so work on the ship was further delayed. It was not until June 1946 that she was towed back to La Ciotat from Etang de Berre, west of Marseilles, where she had been laid up since the summer of 1944. Even then, progress was slow and she was not completed until 1949. In July of that year, she made a short maiden cruise to Naples with Mme. Vincent Auriol,

The largest of the post-War Messageries Maritimes liners, *La Marseillaise* sailed for the French for only eight years.
Laurence Dunn Collection.

Used as a hospital ship during the Suez war of 1956, *La Marseillaise* wore large red crosses on her sides and on her funnel. She is seen anchored just across from the *Henri Poincaré* of Chargeurs Réunis. *Cronican-Arroyo Collection.*

wife of the President of the French Republic, as one of the invited guests. A special commemorative brochure was issued and Messageries Maritimes wrote of their new flagship, "The decoration of *La Marseillaise* – with its choice of bright themes and use of fine materials, carefully selected and meticulously applied – make this vessel a sumptuous palace. The Main Lounge, with its white décor, picked out in tones of red, gold and grey, and enhanced by a richly embroidered tapestry, communicates with the Card Room, walled with lacquer panels, and the Writing Room with dilophane walls and enlivened with monochromes."

The 17,300-ton, 594-foot long *La Marseillaise* was, in her first years, a popular member of the Messageries Maritimes express fleet on the route to the Far East. At first she sailed with such pre-War liners as the *André Lebon*, *Maréchal Joffre*, *Félix Roussel* and the *Athos II*. Later she operated with three brand-new combination liners, the *Cambodge*, *Laos* and *Viet-Nam* of 1952-53. However, as the political situation in Southeast Asia changed, so did the freight and passenger demands for ships such as *La Marseillaise*. Very soon, she was superfluous. Tried in Mediterranean service and then used briefly as a hospital ship during the Suez crisis, she was placed on the sales lists barely eight years after her delivery.

She was purchased by the Arosa Line, a Swiss-based

concern. They were offering 'inexpensive but comfortable' transatlantic crossings as well as winter cruises. Extensively refitted and given a greatly increased passenger capacity, she was renamed *Arosa Sky* and entered service in the spring of 1957. On May 27th, the New York Times reported, "New York welcomed a new liner to port yesterday – the 17,321-ton *Arosa Sky*. As the trim, single-stacked Swiss-owned vessel moved up the Bay with an official welcoming party, she was greeted by the traditional welcoming salutes and fireboat sprays. She was also escorted by helicopters, tugboats and police launches. The black-hulled, triple-screw liner passed the Battery at 9:12 am and tied up at Pier 88, at West 48th Street at 10:20 am." (She would later use Pier 42, at Morton Street.) "Her master expressed complete satisfaction with her sea-keeping qualities. Gale force winds in the Atlantic caused the motorship to be a day late in arriving from German and Channel ports. The captain said that at the height of the storm, he was forced to slow to 8 knots. Large white patches where rough seas had torn away black hull paint on the liner's stem bore witness to the storm. Among the ship's 85 passengers was the Mayor of Arosa, Switzerland, for which the Arosa Line is named. He was delighted with the warmth of the welcome from the world's largest city to a ship that is named after the smallest town in Switzerland (population 3,000). The *Arosa Sky* debarked 755 passengers at Halifax, her last port of call prior to New York."

The *Arosa Sky* now sailed on the North Atlantic in the peak season months, between April and November – trading between Bremerhaven, Le Havre, Southampton, Halifax and New York. She carried just 64 in First Class and 834 in Tourist Class. Beginning in December 1957, she cruised in the winter, off-season. Unfortunately, while she was on an 18-day Grand Caribbean cruise, a fire broke out in some of her passenger cabins. The unpleasant publicity for the Arosa Line was compounded by reports of unclean conditions on the company's ships, unhappy crew members who felt they were inadequately paid and repeated tales of generally unsafe conditions. Reservations for many sailings were lower than anticipated. Matters grew steadily worse and by October 1958 the *Arosa Sky*,

the company's flagship, went back onto the sales list.

Within a month, she was bought by the Costa Line of Genoa who renamed her *Bianca C.* They enlarged her accommodation still further, this time to 202 in First Class and 1,030 in Tourist, and increased her tonnage to 18,427. In a refit which cost well over $2 million, her public rooms and cabins were remodelled in superb contemporary Italian style. She traded on the mid-Atlantic run, between Genoa and the West Indies and on to Venezuela. She also made some winter cruises to the same tropic ports, at first from New York and then from Port Everglades. Unfortunately, she fell victim to a malady well known to French and French-built liners – fire. She burnt off St. George, Granada, and then heeled over and finally sank on October 24th 1961. So ended her very varied career.

The former *La Marseillaise* arrives in New York for the first time as the Arosa Line's new flagship, *Arosa Sky*, in May 1957. On this occasion she berthed at the French Line terminal, Pier 88 at West 48th Street. In the background are the towers of Lower Manhattan, then the hub of the city's financial and shipping industries. *Richard K. Morse Collection.*

Ferdinand de Lesseps, Jean Laborde, Pierre Loti and La Bourdonnais

This quartet was designed especially for the service to East Africa and the Indian Ocean. The *Ferdinand de Lesseps* and the *Jean Laborde* were completed by the Forges et Chantiers de la Gironde at Bordeaux in 1952. During the same year, the *Pierre Loti* came from the Brest Naval Dockyard. Finally, *La Bourdonnais* (seen here) followed in 1953, from the Naval Dockyard at Lorient. At 10,900

tons each, these 17-knot motorships had space for 240 passengers – 88 in First Class, 112 in Tourist and 40 in Third – plus six holds of freight. They were usually routed from Marseilles via the Suez Canal to Djibouti, Mombasa, Dar-es-Salaam, Majunga, Diego Suarez, Tamatave and Mauritius. *La Bourdonnais* and the *Ferdinand de Lesseps* were the first to be retired, being sold late in 1968 to Greece's Efthymiadis Lines. *La Bourdonnais* became the *Knossos* for Eastern Mediterranean service. She was, however, disabled by an engine room fire off Cyprus on May 3rd 1973 and had to be towed back to Piraeus. Never repaired, she was sold to Spanish breakers in 1976. *Eric W. Johnson Collection.*

The 17-knot *Ferdinand de Lesseps* became the *Delphi* for Efthymiadis Lines in late 1968. Used in Eastern Mediterranean service for a time, she was reported to have been sold to Spanish breakers in the spring of 1974. However, she was, in fact, still laid up in Greece in 1977 when Efthymiadis Lines collapsed. The *Delphi* was sold by auction to the Cyprus-based Perla Cruises and became their *La Perla*. The venture was not a success and in 1980 she was sold to another Cypriot company, Intercruise Limited. They renamed her *La Palma*. For a time, she was popular for her Mediterranean fly-cruise holidays. In 1996, however, Intercruise slipped into bankruptcy and the ship was laid up in Perama Bay. There was a suggestion that she would be reactivated for a series of cruises for a British travel trade company, but they lost interest in her and, at the time of writing, she is still idle. She is the last survivor of the onetime Messageries Maritimes East African foursome. *Eric W. Johnson Collection and James Shaw Collection.*

The *Pierre Loti* also went to Efthymiadis, but in 1970. She became the *Olimpia* and then, in 1972, was renamed *Patra*. She was rebuilt for passenger-car ferry service between Brindisi and Patras, assigned to an Efthymiadis associate, the Hellenic Italian Line. It is in this guise that we see her in this photograph. She changed hands again in 1978, sold to Ultramar Armadora (Navieros) SA and renamed *Chrysovalandou II*. A year later, there was a further change and she passed into the ownership of interests known as the Amelia Martin Cia. She became the *Eros* and continued in Mediterranean service. *Luís Miguel Correia.*

Laid up in a damaged condition at Eleusis in Greece during her final years, the *Eros* was sold to local scrappers in 1986 and broken up at Kynosoura. *Steffen Weirauch.*

The *Jean Laborde* was the last to be sold, going to Efthymiadis in 1970. She was first used in local Aegean trades as the *Mykinai* and then, a year later, became the *Ancona* for Adriatic service. She was to have been rebuilt as a ferry, but these plans went astray. In 1974, she became the *Brindisi Express*, but soon afterward was chartered for a cruise-jet service between Singapore and Fremantle in Western Australia under the name *Eastern Princess*. Passengers were flown out from Britain to Singapore and then continued their journey by sea. Troubled by mechanical problems, the ship returned to Greek waters in the summer of 1976. She was eventually sold to Epirotiki Lines and was rebuilt as their 800-capacity cruiseship *Oceanos*. Over the years, she cruised the Mediterranean, the Caribbean, to South America and to Scandinavia and even did a stint on charter to Italy's Lauro Lines. She met a tragic, very dramatic end, however. During a charter cruise voyage off the South African coast between East London and Durban, she began to leak and then flood and her engines were disabled. She sank in rough seas on the afternoon of August 4th 1991. All passengers and crew had been rescued by the South African Air Force and by other ships, including the container vessel *Nedlloyd Mauritius*. *Alex Duncan and Luís Miguel Correia.*

This artist's rendering of the *Viet-Nam* was released in December 1952. Reports claimed that the ship and her two sisters would be the finest set of combo liners built in France since the War. The painting is not quite accurate – the ships actually had large grilled apertures in their funnels, intended to create a flow of air which would carry the smoke from the engines clear of the after decks. *Cronican-Arroyo Collection.*

Cambodge, Laos and Viet-Nam

As we have seen, Messageries Maritimes adopted rather eccentric square-funnelled designs for their passenger ships in the 1920s and 1930s and traditional, sometimes almost overbearing Oriental styles for their interiors. But in post-War years they looked instead to the contemporary, almost to the moderne. By now, their main interest lay with combination passenger-cargo liners. They built three for the Marseilles – Far East service, two to run to the South Pacific and Australia, and a quartet for Mauritius and the Indian Ocean. The trio for the Orient were perhaps the finest and certainly the best-looking. Named for the three states of French Indo-China, they came into service in 1952-54 as the *Viet-Nam*, *Cambodge* and *Laos*.

Built in French shipyards at La Ciotat and Dunkirk, they were good-sized ships for their day – 13,200 tons and 532 feet in length. They were painted completely in white and were capped by all-white, domed single stacks. Masts, booms and hatches for freight were both fore and aft. They carried general cargo outwards, mainly lots of French manufactured goods, including automobiles, as well as the

all-important mail. Homewards, their manifests included the likes of timber, tinned fish, rubber, latex, palm oil, silk and the early mass produced goods coming out of the East. Fast ships powered by steam turbines, they often exceeded their 21 knot service speed to maintain their monthly sailing schedule from Marseilles. They were routed to Port Said, the Suez Canal, Aden, Djibouti, Bombay, Colombo, Singapore, Saigon, Manila, Hong Kong, Kobe and then in reverse at Yokohama.

In their passenger quarters, the company opted for modern styles. On the *Viet-Nam*, for example, the main lounge in First Class was done in soft colors and highlighted by vividly painted Chinese dragons. The floors were inlaid and this space adjoined a small music room. Folding doors in the bar could be opened, giving it a true tropical flavor, certainly one reminiscent of French Saigon. Other facilities included a small writing room, a verandah and a blue tiled outdoor pool that could be floodlit at night. The dining room was notable especially for its descending stairwell, a design feature so often used by the French and used so well. As in second class, the first class restaurant doubled as an evening cinema.

All of the First Class staterooms had private bathrooms (with at least a shower and toilet) and were praised in travel journals for their detailed, thoughtful outfitting – such features as a luggage rack, a folding chair which fitted into a flush position when not in use, reading lamps which could be adjusted to various angles and elevations, extra-wide beds and, unusually for the 1950s, telephones instead of call buttons. Also notably for those days, quite a number of the staterooms had their own private balconies. Importantly on such a hot weather route, there was partial air-conditioning.

In later years, as the passenger trade began to wane, the Messageries Maritimes voyages to the east were included in long, around-the-world tours using three or four different ships. I recall a teacher of mine in the 1960s travelling from New York to Cannes on the *Independence*, then joining the *Cambodge* at Marseilles for the long run out to Hong Kong and then catching the *President Wilson* homewards to San Francisco. In all, the trip took 75 days and the total fare came to about $1,500. But the French Far Eastern run suffered as a result of independence for the colonies in Indo-China. Also, the closure of the Suez Canal in the late 1960s meant that the ships had to be rerouted around South Africa, via Cape Town and Durban. In addition, increasing airline competition and the loss of cargo traffic to the first generation containerships meant that the service's days were indeed numbered.

The *Viet-Nam* became the *Pacifique* in 1968. But time was running out. By 1970, all three sisters were retired. The *Cambodge* was the most fortunate, being sold to the Greek-owned Sun Line and then rebuilt as the cruiseship *Stella Solaris*. She resumed sailing in June 1973 with 765 all-First class berths and much of her original cargo space now given over to passenger quarters. By 1995, she was dividing her time between summers in the Aegean and Eastern Mediterranean and the rest of the year in Caribbean and South American waters.

The *Pacifique* and *Laos* were far less fortunate. They were sold in 1970 to Compañía Navigeción Abeto SA, a Panamanian-flag firm with interests in the Moslem pilgrim trades as well as in Far Eastern service. The *Pacifique* was renamed *Princess Abeto* and was rebuilt at Hong Kong with space for 1,612 passengers, most of them in austere pilgrim quarters. She was soon renamed *Malaysia Baru* and then *Malaysia Kita* for sailings between Singapore and Jeddah. She caught fire on May 12th 1974 while undergoing repairs at Singapore. After being towed to the outer harbor, she sank. Salvage proved difficult and it was not until the summer of 1975 that she was raised. It was nearly another year before she was towed to Taiwanese breakers at Kaohsiung. The *Laos*, too, succumbed to fire. She had been rebuilt as the *Empress Abeto* with a capacity of 1,690 and later sailed as the *Malaysia Raya*. But while at Port Kelang on August 24th 1976, she suffered a devastating blaze. Like her sister, she ended up in the hands of Kaohsiung scrappers.

The 13,162-ton *Viet-Nam*, launched in October 1951, was the first of this splendid trio for Messageries Maritimes' Europe – Far East run.
Eric W. Johnson Collection.

On November 28th 1952, the almost completed *Viet-Nam* was the first ship to enter the new floating dock at Marseilles. She was about to be fitted with her stabilizers. The dock, which could take vessels of up to 40,000 tons, had been provided by the West German government as part of their war reparations to the French.
Cronican-Arroyo Collection.

The fire-ravaged, salvaged remains of the *Malaysia Kita*, the former *Viet-Nam*, as seen at Singapore in 1976.
Steffen Weirauch.

The second of the trio was the *Cambodge*, built at Dunkirk and completed in July 1953. *Eric W. Johnson Collection.*

Rebuilt in 1971-73, the former *Cambodge* reappeared as the greatly altered and very successful Sun Lines cruiseship *Stella Solaris*. *Luís Miguel Correia.*

The 532-foot long *Laos* was the last of this notable trio. She was completed in the summer of 1954. *Alex Duncan*

The former *Laos* as the ill-fated pilgrim ship *Malaysia Raya*. *Hisashi Noma Collection.*

Caledonien and Tahitien

Two further sisterships were built for Messageries Maritimes in the early 1950s, this pair being intended for the service to the French possessions in the South Pacific. The first of the pair, the 12,700-ton, 17-knot *Caledonien*, is shown being launched at Dunkirk on April 26th 1952. With accommodations for 71 passengers in First Class, 84 in Tourist and 86 in so-called Steerage, she was routed from Marseilles via Algiers, Madeira, Guadeloupe, Martinique and then the Panama Canal to Papeete, Port Vila and Noumea, before proceeding to Sydney. With a third ship also employed on the route, there were sailings from Marseilles every six weeks. *Cronican-Arroyo Collection.*

The *Caledonien*, like several of her fleet-mates, was sold to Efthymiadis Lines. In 1972 she became their *Nisos Kypros* and soon thereafter *Island of Cyprus*. Used in Eastern Mediterranean service, her new career was short-lived, however. She was broken-up within three years, in 1975. *Antonio Scrimali.*

First Class onboard the *Tahitien*, like that on her twin sister, was of a very fine standard. There were four de luxe suites and they, and all the cabins, had private bathrooms. The Dining Room was air-conditioned and the amenities included an outdoor swimming pool. The Tourist Class cabins were all outside. Steerage passengers were mostly housed in 8-berth cabins.
Eric W. Johnson Collection.

The *Tahitien* was sold to Cypriot buyers, Aphrodite Cruises Ltd., in 1972 and then rebuilt as the *Atalante*. Refitted with a capacity for 659 passengers, she sailed under the banner of the Med Sun Lines. In 1991, she was chartered to Epirotiki Lines for a time, sailing as their *Homericus*. She reverted to *Atalante* later that same year. She remains in Mediterranean service, one of the last survivors of those notable French combo ships from the early 1950s.
Med Sun Lines.

Mélanésien

Messageries Maritimes also used chartered tonnage on their Pacific passenger service. In 1958, they placed the *Mélanésien* on the route, a 9,500-tonner which had been the Rotterdam Lloyd's *Indrapoera*, a veteran of the old colonial trade to the Dutch East Indies. She had been rebuilt with a capacity of 180 in two classes. She was now owned by the Italian-flag Costa Line, but had been chartered to another Italian firm, the Cogedar Line, who re-chartered her to Messageries Maritimes. When this arrangement ended in 1963, the 38-year old ship was sold to Italian breakers. *Alex Duncan.*

Océanien

Another passenger-cargo ship chartered by Messageries Maritimes was the 10,700-ton former Holland America Line *Noordam* of 1938. Owned by Panamanian-flag owners, Cielomar SA, she was renamed *Océanien* – although it had originally been intended that she be called *Wallisien*. She left Marseilles on her first sailing on the South Pacific route on August 2nd 1963. She lasted until 1967, going to Yugoslavian breakers that winter. *Alex Duncan.*

Polynésie

The small, 3,709-ton *Polynésie* was built at Nantes in 1955 for local Pacific service, sailing between Sydney, Noumea and the New Hebrides. Along with three holds for cargo, she could carry 36 passengers, all in one class. She was the last passenger ship to remain in Messageries Maritimes service, sailing for twenty years and making her last trip from Sydney in October 1975. *Alex Duncan.*

In 1976, after a year's lay up, the *Polynésie* was sold to the Guan Guan Shipping Co. of Singapore and renamed *Golden Glory*. She seems, however, to have been used very little and spent long periods in and around Singapore. She was sold to Taiwanese breakers in the summer of 1979. In this view, we see her at Singapore on November 1st 1978.
Steffen Weirauch.

Pasteur In 1962, in a government-inspired consolidation, Messageries Maritimes took over some of the other French long-distance passenger ship services. At about the same time, the company announced plans for but one more combination ship. Of 18,000 tons, she was to be called *Australien* and was to replace the *Caledonien* and *Tahitien* on the long-distance South Pacific service. But plans soon changed and the ship emerged as the *Pasteur* for the company's newly-acquired Northern Europe – South America run. She entered service in October 1966. She had exceptionally luxurious accommodations for 163 in First Class and 266 in Tourist Class and was rated at the time as the finest passenger liner sailing on the northern run to Latin America. She was routed from Hamburg, Antwerp and Le Havre to Rio, Santos, Montevideo and Buenos Aires. Her European ports were later changed to Hamburg, Le Havre, Southampton and Dunkirk. But aircraft competition soon spelled her end. Her last trip was in October 1972 and she was soon sold to the Shipping Corporation of India as the *Chidambaram*. Her original cargo space was gutted and her passenger capacity quadrupled – to 154 in Cabin Class and 1,526 in dormitories. She was used afterward on the low-fare run between Madras and Singapore. Unfortunately, on February 12th 1985, she was swept by fire in the Bay of Bengal. Fifty people were lost. Damaged beyond repair, the *Chidambaram*'s ruined remains were towed to Bombay and scrapped.
Roger Sherlock.

3
Compagnie Maritime des Chargeurs Réunis

Kerguélen and Jamaïque
Chargeurs Réunis were among the most important of the French shipowners. Based at Le Havre, they operated freighters and passenger ships on routes to South America, West Africa and the Far East. The *Kerguélen* (seen here) and her running-mate *Jamaïque* were built by Swan, Hunter in 1922. They originally belonged to the Cie. Sud-Atlantique – the former having been the *Meduana* until transferred to Chargeurs Réunis in 1928; the latter sailed as *Mosella*, also until 1928 when she

too went to Chargeurs and was renamed. 10,000-ton sisters, they served on the South American run. The *Kerguélen* was seized by the Nazis and used as the *Winrich von Kniprode* until returned to the French in 1945. She reverted to her original name and had a further spell on the South American route before being transferred to the Far Eastern passenger run. By then a vintage ship, she was broken up at Antwerp in 1955. The *Jamaïque* had been broken up at Ghent the year before.   *Captain J. F. van Puyvelde.*

Claude Bernard and Lavoisier   After the War, the French government offered construction subsidies to many national shipowners, including Chargeurs Réunis. An order for a pair of combination passenger-cargo liners, to be named after French scientists, was given in late 1945 to Ateliers et Chantiers de la Loire at St. Nazaire. The plans called for two 11,900-tonners, which would have space for 94 passengers in very fine First Class accommodations and 230 in more spartan Third Class. The *Lavoisier* (shown departing from Lisbon) was launched in October 1948 and completed in the fall of 1950. The *Claude Bernard* was launched that October as well, but was completed six months earlier, in March 1950. They had about twelve years on the North Europe – East Coast of South America run.   *Luís Miguel Correia.*

The *Claude Bernard* and her sister were praised for their fine passenger quarters. Unusually for the time, all cabins in First Class had private bathrooms while most of those in Third Class had their own toilets. There were excellent separate restaurants, an outdoor terrace, a swimming pool and partial air-conditioning. The *Claude Bernard* was sold in 1962 to the East German government-owned Deutsche Seereederei and became the merchant training ship *J. G. Fichte*. Finally retired in 1979, she was sold to a Panama-flag company and became *Sunrise IV* and then *Pegancia*. She was broken up at Karachi in the spring of 1981. *Richard Faber Collection.*

The 537-foot long *Lavoisier* was sold, in August 1961, to Italian buyers new to the passenger trades, Commerciale Marittima Petroli of Palermo. They had her completely rebuilt as the 600-passenger cruiseship *Riviera Prima*, as seen here. At first, she was chartered mostly to the New York-based Caribbean Cruise Lines. When they collapsed, she was sold again, in October 1964, to Norwegian buyers, Berge Sigval Bergesen. Refitted as the *Viking Princess*, she sailed under the banner of Viking Cruise Lines until damaged by a fire in the Caribbean on April 8th 1966. Her charred remains were later towed to Spain for scrapping. *John O'Leary.*

Louis Lumière

A third ship, similar to the *Lavoisier* and *Claude Bernard* but with a more modern funnel, was commissioned in October 1952. Called *Louis Lumière*, she completed the so-called 'Savant class', all named after famous French scholars. She had similar accommodations to the two earlier ships, but with berthing arranged for 109 in First Class and 302 in Third Class. *Alex Duncan.*

During 1962, in an effort to reduce costs, Messageries Maritimes took over the South American passenger services of Chargeurs Réunis and the associated Compagnie de Navigation Sud-Atlantique. The ships were repainted in Messageries Maritimes' white livery, as seen here as the *Louis Lumière* arrives at Lisbon. *Luís Miguel Correia.*

In 1967, the 12,358-ton *Louis Lumière* followed some of her Messageries Maritimes fleetmates and went to Far Eastern owners registered in Panama, Compañía de Navegación Abeto. Renamed *Mei Abeto*, she was reconstructed for the pilgrim trade and could now carry 415 in cabins and 622 deck passengers. She sailed under charter to an Indonesian company, Arafat Lines, who used her on the run from Indonesia to Jeddah. Mechanically troubled in later years (and shown while undergoing lengthy repairs at the Hong Kong United Dockyard),

she was laid up at Djakarta in July 1977. She sat at her moorings for seven years before going to Bangladeshi shipbreakers in May 1984. *Hisashi Noma Collection.*

Edouard Branly, Henri Poincaré and Clément Ader

These three sisters were built at St. Nazaire in the early 1950s. At some 11,300-tons and driven by Sulzer diesels, they were not only smaller, but also less elaborate than most of the other French combination passenger-cargo liners of the post-war era. They were based at Marseilles for the long-distance route out to Indo-China via the Suez Canal. While the actual figures varied slightly from ship to ship, their berthing was generally arranged as some 90 in First Class, 50 or so in Second Class and then about 400 in Third. Here we

see the *Edouard Branly*. But the Indo-China trade was changing and in 1957 all three were sold to the Italian Line. All but 12 of their passenger berths were removed and they were renamed *Antonio Pacinotti*, *Galileo Ferraris* and *Alessandro Volta* respectively. They were placed on the Italian Line's service to the North American West Coast via the Caribbean and Panama. In 1973-74, they were transferred within the government-controlled Finmare group to the Lloyd Triestino and placed on the Italy – East Africa run. All were scrapped in Italy in 1979. *Captain J. F. van Puyvelde.*

Brazza and Foucauld

Completed in 1948, these were the first post-war passenger ships for Chargeurs Réunis. Owing to the devastation of many French shipyards, they had to be built in Britain (by Swan, Hunter & Wigham Richardson at Newcastle and at Wallsend, respectively). At just over 9,000 tons and 479 feet in length, they carried 124 passengers in First Class, 78 in Second Class, 38 Third and 236 in Fourth Class. Latterly with air-conditioning in their main public rooms, they had very comfortable First and Second Class quarters and contemporary décor. They traded from Bordeaux to French West and Equatorial Africa – to Dakar, Conakry, Sassandra, Abidjan, Lome, Cotonou, Douala, Libreville, Port Gentil and Pointe Noire. En route, they also called at Vigo, Leixões or Lisbon and at Madeira or Las Palmas. Here we see the *Brazza*. *Luís Miguel Correia.*

Chargeurs Réunis ended their West African passenger service in 1967. The *Brazza* had already joined the French Navy, becoming their *Maurienne*. Now the *Foucauld* was also transferred and became the Navy's South Pacific transport *Moselle*. Here we see her, though, in her civilian days. A decade later, in August 1977, I recall seeing her passing through the Panama Canal, returning to France to be decommissioned. Both she and the *Maurienne* have since been scrapped. *Luís Miguel Correia.*

Général Leclerc

This 9,500-tonner joined the previously-named pair on the French West African run in 1951. She was very similar to the *Brazza* and *Foucauld*, but, unlike them, was built in France, at St. Nazaire. She was a 16-knot ship, 479 feet long, and had space for 631 passengers – 125 in First Class, 78 in Second, 48 Third Class and 380 Fourth. She too was partially air-conditioned in her later years and had a rather high standard First and Second Class. She was sold off in 1968 and became the Moslem pilgrim ship *Safina-e-Arafat*. She was broken up at Karachi three years later. *Alex Duncan.*

4
Compagnie de Navigation Fraissinet et Cyprien Fabre

Foch

  This was the Fraissinet company's first post-War passenger ship, being completed by Chantiers & Ateliers de St. Nazaire at Penhoet in the summer of 1951. At 9,503 tons and 479 feet in length, she carried 717 passengers – 126 in First Class, 78 Second, 54 Third and 459 troops. She sailed the West African route, from Marseilles to Dakar, Conakry, Abidjan, Takoradi, Lome, Lagos, Duala and Pointe Noire. She greatly resembled the Chargeurs Réunis ships which sailed on a similar route out of Bordeaux. In 1955, Fraissinet merged with the associated Fabre company and then, in 1965, the West African services of Fraissinet, Chargeurs and Paquet were regrouped as Nouvelle Compagnie de Paquebots. Within a year, the *Foch* was sold to the Chinese government, who renamed her *Jian-Hua*. They used her for a time in a service to East Africa. Laid up in 1985, however, she was officially stricken from the active service list two years later. She seems to have been idle for the following decade. In 1997, the Chinese government began to sell off its older tonnage and it is thought that the former *Foch* has by now gone to the breakers. *Cronican-Arroyo Collection.*

Général Mangin Completed in March, 1953, this 12,457-ton ship was an improved, larger version of the *Foch*. Well appointed and completely air-conditioned, she was noted for being the first post-War French passenger-mail ship to be built without state aid. She sailed on the Marseilles – West Africa route until sold to the Chandris group in 1968. They intended to convert her into a cruise ship, but changed their minds and in 1969 sold her to the Philippine President Lines, who renamed her *President*. She was briefly used in service between Manila and Japanese ports. *Cronican-Arroyo Collection.*

She changed hands again, in 1972, going to the Panamanian-registered Compañìa de Navegaciòn Abeto and becoming their *Eastern Queen*. As such, she sailed between Singapore and Fremantle and on other routes. In 1977, she was sold to the Bangaldesh Shipping Corporation and renamed *Hizbul Bahr* for service between Chittagong and Dubai, mainly carrying Bangladeshis going to work in the booming Gulf states. In 1981, she was transferred to the Bangladesh Navy and became the transport, and latterly stationary barracks ship, *Shaheed Salahuddin.*

Luis Miguel Correia Collection.

Jean Mermoz / Mermoz

Four years after the *Général Mangin* was completed, her near-sister, the *Jean Mermoz*, entered service. Here we see her being launched at St. Nazaire on November 17th 1956. She was named after a famous French aviator. *Richard Faber Collection.*

The *Jean Mermoz* was the last passenger ship built for the Fraissinet Line. She sailed in the Marseilles – West African trade until 1970.
W. H. Young & L. A. Sawyer.

Extensively rebuilt at Genoa in 1970 as a full-time cruiseship and now called simply *Mermoz*, the all-one class, 757-passenger ship travelled on worldwide itineraries: the Mediterranean, Scandinavia, the Caribbean, Alaska, the Indian Ocean, etc. By 1984, she was the sole deep-sea passenger ship flying the tricolor, but in that year she was transferred to the Bahamas flag. Latterly, she sailed under the management of Paquet Cruises, who in 1993 became part of the Costa Line of Genoa.
Luís Miguel Correia.

A stern view of the traditionally styled *Mermoz* at Copenhagen on June 5th 1993. By 1999, she was 42 years old and had long been rumored to be for sale. She was bought by the Cypriot-based Louis Cruise Lines and renamed *Serenade*. She now runs short cruises in the Eastern Mediterranean. *Ove Nielsen.*

5

Compagnie de Navigation Mixte

El Mansour

The Cie. de Navigation Mixte was an important operator on the routes from Marseilles and Port Vendres to North Africa. It had an interesting and distinctive fleet, including the 400-foot long *El Mansour*, which by the late 1950s was one of the oldest ships in the North African trade. When she was built at La Seyne in 1933 she had two squat funnels and two masts. After being scuttled at Marseilles by the retreating Nazis in 1944, she was later salvaged and extensively rebuilt (in 1947-48) with a single stack and one mast. At 6,000

tons, she could carry 86 First Class passengers (including 4 travelling de luxe and 12 designated priorité), as well as 202 Tourist Class and 530 deck passengers. A rather powerful ship with a service speed of over 20 knots, she was transferred to the French Navy in 1963 and became the missile-research ship *Maine* based in the South Pacific. She was deliberately sunk in French naval operations in 1973. *Richard Faber Collection.*

Président de Cazalet

The 5,227-ton *Président de Cazalet* and her sister, *Sidi Bel Abbes*, were ordered by the French government from a British shipbuilder, Swan, Hunter & Wigham Richardson, just after the War, in 1946. The *Président de Cazalet* was allotted to the Mixte company. Quite a fast ship, with a service speed of 20 knots, she was commissioned in the summer of 1948 for the North African trade. Her capacity was listed as 2 de luxe, 92 First Class, 226 Tourist and 500 deck passengers. Her orthodox funnel was replaced by one of the Strombos type in 1950. In 1958, during the violent events leading up to Algerian independence, she made headlines when a bomb exploded onboard while she was at sea near Marseilles, killing one and wounding many others. In 1967, she was transferred to CGT and renamed *Méditerranée*. Like many other French passenger ships, she was sold to Efthymiadis Lines of Greece. They bought her in 1971 and called her *Arcadi*. She was used for Mediterranean cruising as well as inter-island sailings within the Aegean, but her owners went into bankruptcy in 1977 and she was laid up in Perama Bay, along with most of her fleetmates. Neglected and beyond re-sale for further service, she was sold to Turkish breakers at Aliaga in 1984. *Richard Faber Collection.*

In this view, the *Arcadi* (ex-*Méditerranée*, ex-*Président de Cazalet*) is moored alongside another Efthymiadis passenger ship, the *Knossos*, which had been *La Bourdonnais* of Messageries Maritimes. They are at Perama in Greece and the year is 1976. *Michael Cassar.*

Djebel-Dira

Completed in 1948, this 4,180-ton vessel was one of several French vessels built in Britain after the Second World War. She came from Swan, Hunter & Wigham Richardson. A rather upright little combination passenger-cargo ship, she was especially suitable for the Marseilles – Casablanca route. Of her four cargo holds, two were insulated for chilled meats, fruit and vegetables and she also carried bulk wine and live sheep. Her accommodations were arranged for 56 First Class, 132 Third and 430 deck passengers. *Alex Duncan.*

Like many other French passenger ships at the time, the 371-foot long *Djebel-Dira* was sold to Greek buyers in 1970. The purchaser was Spyros P. Billinis, who renamed her *Phoenix*. Stripped of her cargo holds and rebuilt for cruising, she was later renamed *Melody* and sent on voyages to the Greek isles, Turkey and Israel. She was, however, badly damaged in a severe storm while en route to Haifa in December, 1980. She lay unrepaired for many months. Her owners at the time, Athens Marine Cruises, went bankrupt and she passed to the IMS Shipping Co. and then to Cougar Shipping Co., who used Honduran registry. Eventually, she fell into Greek government ownership but when, in July 1990, some repairs were finally underway, she caught fire and began to sink by the stern. Still half-submerged, she remains to this day off Atalanti Island. Nearby is another abandoned cruiseship, the *Bella Maria*, which in earlier days had been the French *Azemmour*. *Antonio Scrimali.*

Kairouan

One of the most fascinating and important ships on the French North African run, this 8,589-tonner was laid down in 1940, soon after the beginning of the War. She was launched a year later, only to be sunk by the retreating Germans at Toulon in 1944. Three years later, she was raised. It was a difficult operation as her stern was resting on another sunken liner, the Italian *Virgilio*. She was finally completed, by Forges et Chantiers de la Méditerranée at La Seyne, in 1950, ten years after her launch. 486 feet long, she was novel in several ways: she had

turbo-electric drive, influenced by the exceptional *Normandie*; she had a Strombos funnel; and, unusually for 1950, all her public rooms and First Class cabins were air-conditioned. She cut 2 hours off the Marseilles to Algiers passage, making it in 17 hours. Her passenger facilities included a cinema. There was a garage and space for either general cargo or fruit and vegetables in her holds. Known to have made 26 knots during her trials, she averaged 24 knots as a service speed. Her 133 First Class berths were actually subdivided into 4 de luxe, 10 priorité, 48 semi-luxe and 71 others. There were also 291 berths in Second Class and she could carry 750 deck passengers. She met her end at the hands of Spanish breakers in late 1973. *Richard Faber Collection.*

El Djezaïr

In the annals of ship construction, the 7,608-ton *El Djezaïr* was an important vessel, the first European-owned passenger ship to have her engines and therefore her funnel placed aft. Over forty years earlier, several American vessels of the Matson Line had used this design. Completed in 1952, the *El Djezaïr* did, however, pre-date Britain's *Southern Cross* of 1955 which is widely acknowledged as the first modern liner with this configuration. Used in the Marseilles – North Africa trade, the 21-knot *El Djezaïr* had quarters for 124 First Class and 220 Tourist, as well as 650 deck passengers. Fitted with a Strombos funnel, she had a chapel and a cinema. Her turbines had actually been salvaged from a previous ship of the same name, which had been built in 1934 but had been sunk by the Germans in 1944. The post-War *El Djezaïr* had a relatively short career with the Mixte company, being sold in 1969. The buyers were Cypriot-flag owners, Sovereign Cruises, who called her *Floriana* and planned to convert her into a cruiseship. But little work had been done when, in 1971, she passed into the ownership of Chandris Cruises. Their intention was to make her over as a summertime Mediterranean cruiseship, with winters in the Caribbean. But, on closer examination, Chandris engineers found her 37-year old turbines faulty and beyond practical repair. Laid-up for a further two years, she was sold to local scrappers at Perama in Greece in 1973.

Richard Faber Collection.

6
Compagnie de Navigation Paquet

Djenné / Césarée and Koutoubia / Phocée

The Paquet Line occupied a position in the colonial trade from Marseilles to Morocco and West Africa rather similar to that of the old French Line on the North Atlantic run. They both had a certain prestige. The Paquet Line – Compagnie de Navigation Paquet – had a fleet of white, multi-classed passenger ships which sailed out of the Mediterranean and into the Atlantic to such ports as Casablanca, Las Palmas, Tangiers and Dakar. Among the Paquet ships which survived the Second World War were two 8,800-tonners, the *Djenné* and the *Koutoubia*, which had been built at La Seyne in 1931. At that time they had two funnels. Here we see

a wartime picture of the *Koutoubia*. A near-sister, the *Maréchal Lyautey*, was sunk in 1944 and, although raised, never re-entered service. The two surviving ships were both refitted and restyled with a single Strombos-type stack. The accommodations onboard the *Djenné* were grouped for 122 in First Class, 192 in Second, 204 Third and 636 Fourth. In 1960, Paquet created a subsidiary for Eastern Mediterranean service, known as Cie. Française de Navigation. The *Koutoubia* was used first, running Marseilles-Haifa sailings and making occasional cruises. For this new phase in her life, she was renamed *Phocée*. By late 1962, she was replaced by the *Djenné* which now became the *Césarée*. The *Césarée* endured for another three years before being broken up at Split in 1965. *Alex Duncan Collection.*

The *Djenné* docked at Casablanca in 1936. *V. H. Young & L. A. Sawyer Collection.*

Funnel contrasts. First, we see the *Djenné* wearing the CNP colours (Compagnie de Navigation Paquet) and, later, the same ship as the *Césarée*, running to the Eastern Mediterranean for the Compagnie Française de Navigation. *Alex Duncan Collection and Roger Sherlock Collection.*

Azrou and Azemmour

Built by Ateliers et Chantiers de Bretagne at Nantes in 1949 and 1951 respectively, these 3,900-ton combination passenger-cargo ships were used on the France-Morocco run, from Marseilles to Tangier and Casablanca. 16-knot vessels, they measured 373 feet in length and could carry 56 in First Class, 46 in Second Class and between 160 and 240 in Third. They were specially fitted to carry sheep as well as wine in bulk. The *Azemmour* is pictured here. *Alex Duncan Collection.*

Like several other French passenger ships, the *Azrou* and *Azemmour* were sold to Constantinos Efthymiadis of Greece – the *Azrou* in 1968, to become the *Melina*; and the *Azemmour* a year later, to become the *Delos*, as seen here. They were both rebuilt as 500-capacity cruiseships and were fitted with swimming pools, stabilizers, a disco and a nightclub. All cabins were given private facilities. Generally, they were assigned to 7-day cruises from Piraeus to the Greek islands and Turkey. Unfortunately, both ships proved to be mechanically troublesome. Following the collapse of Efthymiadis in 1977 and the seizure of their ships, both the *Delos* and the *Melina* were laid up. *Roger Sherlock.*

The *Melina* was scrapped at Perama in Greece in 1980. *Antonio Scrimali.*

Just before the *Melina* (ex-*Azrou*) was scrapped, her engines were removed and placed aboard the *Delos* (ex-*Azemmour*). Shortly afterwards, in 1980, the *Delos* was sold to the Aquaviva Shipping Co. and renamed *Bella Maria* for cruising in the Adriatic. But after only her second sailing, she developed serious engine troubles at Patras and had to be towed to Piraeus. She was soon laid up. *Luís Miguel Correia.*

At the time of writing, the *Bella Maria* (ex-*Azemmour*) lies abandoned outside Piraeus harbor, not far from Atalanti Island. *Antonio Scrimali.*

Lyautey / Galilée

This 9,931-ton, 1952-built ship was one of the most important members of the French African passenger fleet in the 1950s and 1960s. Completed at La Seyne in 1952, she was quite fast, with a service speed of 22 knots (24.5 knots during her sea trials). Until the 14,200-ton *Ancerville* appeared in the late summer of 1962, the *Lyautey* was Paquet's largest passenger ship to date. Her 465-foot long hull and her upperworks seemed to be dominated by her Strombos-type funnel. She could carry 20 passengers in de luxe accommodations, 192 in so-called Confort Class, 211 in

Tourist and 122 in Third Class. There was also provision for 220 troops. Most of her public rooms were air-conditioned. During a 1963 refit, stabilizers and an outdoor pool were added and the cabins were modernized and upgraded.

She sailed in regular services from Marseilles, either to Casablanca and the Canary Islands; or to Casablanca and Dakar, returning via the Canaries. The passage time between Marseilles and Casablanca was a quick 40 hours, to Dakar 100 hours. In later years, she was partnered by the larger *Ancerville*.

In 1965, she was transferred to Paquet's Eastern Mediterranean subsidiary, Cie. Française de Navigation, and was renamed *Galilée*. Competing with the ships of Israel's Zim Lines, she sailed primarily between Marseilles and Haifa. She later returned to her old routes to the west coast of Africa, by now running for the newly created Nouvelle Compagnie de Paquebots in which Paquet still had a partial interest. It was reported in 1966 that she had been sold to Italian buyers to become the *Margarita*. But this never came to pass. Instead, in 1967, she joined Greece's Efthymiadis Lines and was renamed *Lindos*. Used mainly between Piraeus and Cyprus, often via Rhodes, she was eventually retired and was broken up in 1975. *Richard Faber Collection.*

Ancerville

Certainly one of the most interesting of the French African liners, Paquet's *Ancerville* was completed in 1962 by Chantiers de l'Atlantique at St. Nazaire. She followed the giant *France* from that same yard. Launched in April, she was commissioned a few months later, in September. She was designed for the Marseilles – Morocco – Canary Islands – Senegal service, but was made easily convertible for one-class cruising. On the African run, her accommodations were arranged for 171 in First Class, 346 in Tourist and 253 in Third Class. Powered by Burmeister & Wain diesels, she was typically fast, with a service speed of 22.5 knots. *World Ship Society.*

With the African trades declining and the costs of operating French-flag passenger ships escalating, the 551-foot long *Ancerville* was sold in April 1973 to COSCO, the China Ocean Shipping Company, who renamed her *Minghua*. At first used in government service between China and East Africa, she did some unsuccessful Australian and South Pacific charter cruising in the early 1980s. Her accommodations were then listed as 380, all in First Class. By 1986, however, she was removed from active service and was converted into a permanently moored hotelship at Shenzhen in China. She remains there at the time of writing. *Roger Sherlock.*

Renaissance

Launched in December 1965 for Paquet's subsidiary Cie. Française de Navigation, the 11,724-ton *Renaissance* was an outstanding vessel from the start. Initially intended for the Marseilles – Eastern Mediterranean route, she began cruising soon afterward and was later used in North European waters, in the North American market (cruising to the Caribbean, Alaska, around South America from Florida, etc.). She became noted for her outstanding Music At Sea Festival cruises. She had accommodations for 416 passengers. Like so many others, she was a costly ship to operate and so, in 1977, this elegant liner was sold to Greece's Epirotiki Lines, who renamed her *Homeric Renaissance*. However, Epirotiki soon placed her on long-term charter to Costa Cruises of Genoa and she sailed for them as the *World Renaissance*. Later, she made cruises for Epirotiki themselves. In the summer of 1995, she was sold once again, this time to Indonesian buyers, the Club Awani Travel Group, who used her for cruises from Djakarta as the *Awani Dream*. However, in 1998 she reverted to Epirotiki, who had meanwhile merged with another Greek company, the Sun Line, to become Royal Olympic Cruises. She was once again called *World Renaissance* and resumed European cruising.
Port Authority of Le Havre.

Massalia

Completed by the Dubigeon-Normandie shipyard at Nantes in 1971, this 10,513-tonner was built for the Nouvelle Compagnie de Paquebots, successors to the Paquet Line. She was intended to carry cars and passengers in their Marseilles – Casablanca – Canary Islands service and was typical of a whole class of such ships which Dubigeon built for various owners. She was fitted to carry 494 First Class and 316 Tourist passengers and 260 cars. In late 1983, however, she was sold off, going to the Swedish-flag Stena Line. Within a year, she went through three changes

of name – *Stena Baltica*, *Island Fiesta* (for short cruises out of Florida ports) and *Scandinavian Star* (for Florida's SeaEscape Cruises). *Michael D. J. Lennon.*

On March 16th 1988, the *Scandinavian Star* suffered a serious engine room fire when some 60 miles off the Mexican coast and was eventually towed to Miami for major repairs. However, further tragedy struck her on April 7th 1990. Since March, she had been chartered to the Da-No Line for ferry service between Frederikshavn and Oslo. On her fifth trip, she made international headlines. A fire started by an arsonist proved to be one of the worst of its kind in history. At first, it was reported that all aboard were safe. In fact, at least 160 perished, including the Da-No Line's former owner and his wife. It was also reported that language difficulties arose between the diverse nationalities amongst the passengers and crew and that this soon led to chaos. In the end, it was an 'every man for himself' situation.

Following the fire and an initial lay up in Sweden, the 466-foot long *Scandinavian Star* was moved to a Copenhagen shipyard for a criminal investigation by the Danish authorities. Then, in August 1990, she was towed across the North Sea to Hull, appraised by ship repairers and provisionally renamed *Candi*. A month later, she was moved to Southampton to await possible buyers. In fact, she was not sold until February 1994,

when she went for $2million to International Shipping Partners who placed her under the Bahamian flag. That summer, she was sent to La Spezia and was rebuilt with accommodations for 385 passengers in cabins and 70 deck passengers. She was now called the *Regal Voyager*. In the spring of 1995, she was transferred to a firm called St. Thomas Cruises. Soon, however, she was chartered to the Isabel Cortes Ferry Service Ltd. for weekly voyages between Port Isabel, Texas and Puerto Cortes in Honduras. At weekends she runs one-day gambling cruises from Port Isabel to the nearby Casino Isabella. The *Regal Voyager* is now listed as having accommodations for 456 passengers. *Luís Miguel Correia.*

Azur This car-carrying ferry was also built by Dubigeon-Normandie at Nantes – but for British owners, the General Steam Navigation Co., a P & O subsidiary. Completed in 1971, she was called *Eagle*. A large ferry for her time (11,609 gross tons), she could carry 740 passengers and some 200 vehicles. She was used on the 'sunshine run' between Southampton, Lisbon and Tangier. Soon, she was transferred to another P & O company, Southern Ferries Ltd., but was unsuccessful. In December 1975, she was sold to the Nouvelle Cie. de Paquebots and became the *Azur*. They used her for the Marseilles – West African service as well as for Mediterranean cruising; and in 1981, she was converted for full-time cruising with her capacity increased to 1,039. By 1983, her tonnage was relisted as 14,717 gross. But Paquet's standards had slipped. Lewis Gordon, who had previously enjoyed superb food on the *Mermoz*, was extremely disappointed to find that on the *Azur* "the food was for peasants. We had hamburger meat every night." In early 1987, the ship changed hands again, sold to Panamanian-flag buyers, the Azur Transportation Co. They amended her name slightly, to *The Azur*, and chartered her to Chandris Cruises, who sailed her in the Mediterranean in the summer and in the Caribbean (and later in West African waters) in winter. When this charter expired in 1994, she was transferred to another Mediterranean operator, Festival Cruises. *Steffen Weirauch.*

The Azur of Festival Cruises, with her characteristic Dubigeon side-by-side twin funnels, is seen here berthed at Genoa. *Antonio Scrimali.*

Rhapsody Holland America Line's 24,200-ton, 952-passenger *Statendam*, completed in the winter of 1957 for a dual purpose – North Atlantic service between Rotterdam and New York and winter, off-season cruising – was sold to Paquet Cruises in the fall of 1981. Now registered in the Bahamas and using a multinational crew, she was renamed *Rhapsody* and sailed in summer from Vancouver to Alaska and for the remainder of the year in the Caribbean. She and the *Mermoz* were marketed in North America at the time as "Paquet French Cruises". French cuisine and style were emphasized. But with troublesome engines and increasing competition within the American cruise business, the *Rhapsody*'s days were clearly numbered. Then, in 1984, she ran aground off Grand Cayman and was only saved with great difficulty. In 1986, after only five years with Paquet, she was sold to Greece's Regency Cruises and renamed *Regent Star* (seen here during a transit of the Panama Canal). Her worn-out turbines were replaced by diesel engines. When Regency collapsed in October 1995, she was laid up in Eleusis Bay, near Piraeus in Greece. Despite rumors of revival, she has since fallen into a badly deteriorated state. Nevertheless, in the summer of 2000 there were rumors of a return to service, but this seemed unlikely. *Regency Cruises.*

7

Compagnie de Navigation Sud-Atlantique

The Mighty Pasteur

On an overcast July morning back in 1959, New York harbor was especially festive. Not only was there a string of outbound liners, including the speedy *United States*, but a new passenger ship, in fact a quite notable one, was due. I took a place at the highest spot in Hoboken, on the hilltop campus of Stevens Institute of Technology, which is directly across from 14th Street in Manhattan, and waited. Soon, the new ship came into view, moving slowly and already escorted by tugs, spraying fireboats and buzzing helicopters. The whistles from harbor craft were sounding their reverent salutes. But the publicists had been especially creative. The outbound *Berlin* would meet and pass the inbound *Bremen*, that new ship arriving on her first visit. It was an historic occasion: the first time that two German liners were at New York together since before World War II, since August 1939. The two ships passed one another off Lower Manhattan, in the shadows of the great towers of the city's financial and shipping districts. It was also a special treat for spectators lining the seawall at Battery Park. In particular, the *Bremen*'s whistles were thunderous and seemed to echo for miles.

Sparkling in fresh paint and rebuilt to defy her true age, the 'new', 699-foot long *Bremen* was, in fact, a ship with an interesting past. She had been the French *Pasteur*, the last big liner to be built at St. Nazaire before the Second World War erupted. Created for the Compagnie de Navigation Sud-Atlantique, she was designed for the South Atlantic run, for the route from Bordeaux down to Rio de Janeiro, Santos, Montevideo and Buenos Aires. She was a slightly smaller replacement for the splendid *L'Atlantique*, a glorious three-stacker which had burned in 1933 when only two years old. The French had to maintain a position in the South American trade and especially to compete with the likes of Britain's brand new *Andes*, Germany's celebrated *Cap Arcona* and Italy's sleek *Neptunia* and *Oceania*. Lavish brochures detailed the *Pasteur*'s opulent quarters, especially in First Class, while one of France's finest marine artists, Albert Brenet was contracted to paint her. A superb poster was issued and today it is a valuable collectible, selling for over $1,000.

But commercial service for the 30,500-ton *Pasteur* never came to pass. Once the War started, in September 1939, the newly-completed liner was shunted off to Brest for safe-keeping, if only temporarily. When France itself was threatened, in the spring of 1940, she was quickly dispatched to Halifax, where she landed large reserves of gold bullion from the government treasuries in Paris. She soon passed into Allied control, being managed by P & O (and later by Cunard-White Star). She came to New York for the first time in June 1940, tying-up on the south side of French Line's Pier 88 and just across from the giant *Normandie* and another new liner, the *Queen Elizabeth*. Painted over in gray, the *Pasteur* was soon off to war, sailing out east. Later, by 1943, she returned to the Atlantic and carried thousands of American and Canadian troops over to Scotland for the eventual invasion of Normandy. At this time, she often sailed in tandem with a French 'cousin' of sorts, the famous *Ile de France*.

Then the largest French liner for the South American trade, the *Pasteur* lies just across from the largest French North Atlantic liner, the *Normandie*. The *Queen Elizabeth* is in the upper right-hand corner. The French ships are lying at New York's Pier 88 and the date is June 16th 1940.
Cronican-Arroyo Collection.

Hailed as the World's biggest troopship, the _Pasteur_ is seen as she passes through the locks at Ijmuiden in Holland on February 24th 1950. Bound for Amsterdam, she had been specially chartered by the Dutch government to bring 4,000 soldiers back from Indonesia. *Cronican-Arroyo Collection.*

Cunard master Eric Ashton-Irvine recalled the _Pasteur_. "We had taken her over at Halifax, where Nazi sympathisers had actually tried to sink her. She was one of my least favorite ships. She was not a good sea boat. She rolled enormously, had a rather shallow draft (30 feet) and

her huge funnel caused wind problems. Within, there were especially low ceilings and too many interconnecting cabins and glass-mirrored bathrooms – which were confusing, to say the least."

When the War ended in 1945, it was briefly felt that

the *Pasteur* would be restored for luxury service. Instead, the French government had other plans and needs: she was used as a full, peacetime trooper, carrying up to 4,000 per voyage. Mainly, she sailed out to colonial Indo-China.

A friend saw the *Pasteur* idle and laid-up in Marseilles in 1956. He was headed for London, inbound from Sydney on the *Orsova*, which had called at the French port to land passengers anxious to cut a few days off their passage and to avoid the notorious Bay of Biscay. He remembered the French ship because of her most distinctive feature, her enormous single funnel. Few ships had greater stacks. It certainly gave the ship a special identity and this was likely the intention of her designers back in the late 1930s. With trooping duties over, there were once again rumors that she would be refitted to luxury standards, this time to be given over to the French Line for sailings to New York as a replacement, if only temporary, for the then thirty year-old *Ile de France*. It did not happen. The new 66,000-ton *France* was already a confirmed project by then and she would replace both the *Ile* and the *Liberté*.

Once the Allied restrictions on German ownership of large passenger ships had been lifted in 1955, the North German Lloyd awoke, eager to restore something of its pre-War Bremerhaven – New York service. The 19,100-ton *Berlin*, the former Swedish American *Gripsholm* of 1925, was quickly acquired, but the Germans wanted something even larger, faster, more luxurious. And so they bought the *Pasteur*, stripped her and gave her a fresh, very contemporary look. She became the two-class *Bremen*, West Germany's new flagship.

When the *Bremen* first visited New York in that summer of 1959, she berthed once again at French Line's Pier 88. In the other berth was the *Liberté*. The New York Times found it to be interesting material for an article: one liner was ex-French and now German, while the other was formerly German and now French. (The *Liberté* had, of course, been the record-breaking superliner *Europa* of 1930.)

The *Bremen* had ten or so good years, divided between Atlantic crossings, cruises out of New York and cruises out of Bremerhaven. She offered fine service, comfortable accommodations and was noted for her immaculate

standards. I did a week-long cruise to Bermuda aboard her in 1968 and especially recall the magnificent place settings in the restaurant with the finest crystal and china, the hand-washed silverware and the whitest of linens. The linoleum floors gleamed like glass and the outer decks were snow-like. She was one of the last ships aboard which I remember shoes being placed outside cabin doors at night so as to be polished by morning. In the rough seas off Cape Hatteras, the 23-knot *Bremen* took a pounding but performed very well.

By 1970, however, mechanical problems and even breakdowns were causing delayed or cancelled sailings. A year later, the Germans decided to pull out of Atlantic liner service and so put the ageing *Bremen* up for sale. The Greeks were then busily buying many older passenger ships and the German flagship seemed appealing to Chandris Cruises. She became their *Regina Magna* and was used for cruising from Amsterdam, London, Genoa and Piraeus, and later in the Caribbean. I did a Baltic capitals trip on her in the summer of 1972 and then a 7-day Caribbean cruise out of Curacao over Christmas 1973. She was still a wonderful ship. But she was fuel-thirsty and therefore an expensive ship to operate, even for clever Greek shipowners like Chandris. After the dramatic fuel oil price increases of 1973, she was laid-up in the backwaters near Piraeus. Nearby was another aged Chandris liner, the 47-year old *Queen Frederica*.

The chances of finding another owner for the *Regina Magna* seemed slim indeed. But in 1977, she was sold to the Philippine Singapore Ports Corporation and was sent off to Jeddah, where she arrived on October 6th. She was renamed *Saudi Phil 1*, flew the Philippine flag and was used as an accommodation ship for up to 3,500 workers, most of them Filipinos brought to Arabia for construction projects. Months later, in March 1978, she changed names yet again, becoming the *Filipinas Saudi I*. This assignment ended by early 1980 and the ship, which had fallen into poor condition, was suitable only for scrapping. The Taiwanese bought her, but en route under tow for Kaohsiung, on June 6th, she sprang a leak and sank in the Indian Ocean. Her bow lifted out of the sea and pointed skyward as she sank stern-first. The career of the *Pasteur*, 'the ship with the big stack' as one friend called her, was over.

Laënnec and Charles Tellier

These sisters were ordered several years after two similar ships, the *Lavoisier* and *Claude Bernard*, which were delivered to the associated Chargeurs Réunis company. The *Laënnec* (shown here) and the *Charles Tellier* came from the same St. Nazaire yard and were delivered in January and July of 1952 respectively. They had the same high standards of accommodation, 110 First Class and 326 Third Class, but equally

important was their five-hold cargo capacity. On the northbound run from the River Plate, they carried considerable amounts of refrigerated beef. Both ships had nearly fifteen years in the South American service, from Hamburg, Antwerp and Le Havre, and then via Vigo, Leixões and Madeira to Rio de Janeiro, Santos, Montevideo and Buenos Aires. *Alex Duncan.*

In 1962, the French services to South America were taken over by Messageries Maritimes and it is in their colors that we see the *Charles Tellier* sailing from Lisbon. She and her sister were eventually sold to Far Eastern buyers in 1966-67. The new owners registered them under the Panamanian flag under the title Compañía de Navegación Abeto. The *Laënnec* became the *Belle Abeto* while the *Charles Tellier* changed to *Le Havre Abeto*. *Luís Miguel Correia.*

Chartered to Arafat Lines, the two ships were mainly used for seasonal sailings in the Muslim pilgrim trade between Djakarta and Jeddah but also made some voyages from Singapore to Hong Kong, Kobe and Yokohama. The *Belle Abeto* (seen here) was refitted to carry 100 cabin passengers and 1,352 pilgrims in

dormitories and on deck; the *Le Havre Abeto* was rearranged for 415 cabin passengers and 610 others. In the end, the *Belle Abeto* (ex-*Laënnec*) was destroyed by fire at Sasebo, Japan on July 30th 1976. Ablaze from end to end, she had to be towed to the outer harbor and deliberately sunk. Soon afterwards, the *Le Havre Abeto* (ex-*Charles Tellier*) was laid up at Djakarta. In poor condition, she was finally sold to Bangladeshi scrappers at Chittagong and delivered to them in June 1984. *Alex Duncan.*

8

Nouvelle Compagnie Havraise Péninsulaire de Navigation

Ile de la Réunion, Ile Maurice and Nossi-Be

In the post-War years, Nouvelle Cie. Havraise Péninsulaire de Navigation ran three 27-passenger combo ships to the islands of the Indian Ocean. The first two, built in 1949 and 1951, came from a Danish yard at Odense while the third was constructed by the French themselves at Le Trait in 1952. At 8,800 tons each, these 16-knot vessels were fitted with ample general cargo spaces as well as refrigerated compartments and tanks for wines. The passenger quarters were of a high standard and all cabins had private bathroom facilities. While their itineraries varied somewhat according to cargo demand, they were usually routed from Hamburg, Antwerp, Dunkirk or Le Havre, Rouen, Algiers and Marseilles via Suez to Djibouti, Majunga, Nossi-Be, Diego Suarez, Tamatave, Mauritius, Réunion and such smaller ports as Mananjary, Manakara, Tulear and Fort Dauphin. In this photograph we see the *Ile Maurice*.

The three sisters remained with the French until 1971-2. The *Ile de la Réunion* was sold to Panamanian-flag buyers, Astroprimo Armadora S/A and renamed *Astree*. According to Peter Eisele, for many years editor of the journal Steamboat Bill, "She was traded to Gulf Shipping in 1976, becoming the Sharjah-flag *Gulf Majesty*. Surprisingly, she found yet another buyer in 1978, being sold to Alvidah Shipping S/A, who renamed her *Guru Angadh*. In 1980, she went to shipbreakers in Taiwan."

"The *Ile Maurice* was also sold to Astroprimo in 1971 and was renamed *Altair*", added Mr. Eisele. "She was sold again, to Prestige Shipping Company of Cyprus in 1973 and then became *Papafotis*. In 1979, she was delivered to Desguances Maritima at Vinaroz, who began scrapping her that April."

"The *Nossi-Be* also traded for Astroprimo, but under the Liberian flag initially, as *Pegase*," he added. "A year later, she changed to the Panama flag. She was sold to Greek buyers and seems to have been fitted for the carriage of bitumen. While northwest of Guernsey on February 27th 1975, she suffered a fire in her accommodation, in which one member of the crew was killed and the ship herself sustained extensive damage. She was towed to Falmouth and put up for sale. She was subsequently sold to S. W. "De Koophandel" and towed to Nieuw Lekkerkerk in Holland for breaking-up, arriving there on April 27th 1975." *Roger Sherlock.*

9
Société Générale
de Transports Maritimes

Florida By the early 1950s, the 9,536-ton *Florida* was the oldest passenger ship in the Transports Maritimes fleet. Built at St. Nazaire in 1926, she sailed the Marseilles – East Coast of South America run. She was, however, badly damaged in 1931 in a collision off Gibraltar with the British aircraft carrier *HMS Glorious*. Later, during the Second World War, she was damaged and sunk at Bone in Algeria. Declared a loss, she was in fact salvaged in 1944 and was thoroughly rebuilt two years later. She now had only one stack instead of the original two. In 1955, she was sold to the Italian shipowners Fratelli Grimaldi who allotted her to their Siosa Line subsidiary. Now called *Ascania*, she sailed the busy emigrant run between the West Indies and England via Spain and Portugal until assigned to full-time Western Mediterranean cruising in 1966. But she was becoming worn out and was sent to the breakers at La Spezia in 1968, by which time she was 42 years old. *Marius Bar and Alex Duncan.*

Campana The 10,816-ton *Campana* was an enlarged version of the *Florida*. Built three years later, in 1929, at one of Swan, Hunter's Tyneside yards, she too sailed in the East Coast of South America trade – from Marseilles out to Rio de Janeiro, Santos, Montevideo and Buenos Aires. After the fall of France in 1940, she was laid up at Buenos Aires and was later seized by the Argentine government. For a time, she was named *Rio Jachal* and ran several Buenos Aires – New Orleans sailings for the Argentine State Line. But in 1946, with the War over, she was handed back to the French, refitted and returned to the Latin American trade. She also made some sailings out to colonial Indo-China for Chargeurs Réunis. *Richard Faber Collection.*

In 1955, the *Campana* was sold, along with the *Florida*, to Grimaldi-Siosa. Renamed *Irpinia*, she was rebuilt at Genoa with a new, raked bow and now with quarters for 1,221 passengers in two classes. Mostly, she

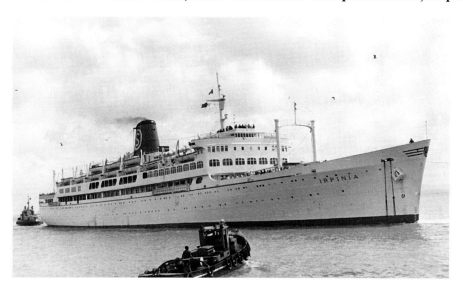

sailed between Europe and the Caribbean, but she also made transatlantic crossings between the Mediterranean and the St.Lawrence River ports of Quebec City and Montreal. In addition, she made some cruises, as well as occasional sailings to New York. In 1962, she was rebuilt even further – the original twin stacks were replaced by a single more streamlined one, new Fiat diesels were fitted and the accommodations were greatly modernized. We see her here, in her restyled state, arriving at Lisbon. *Luís Miguel Correia.*

After 1970, the *Irpinia* sailed as a Mediterranean cruiseship. Also, in 1976, she served as a 'floating set' for the film *Voyage of the Damned*. She portrayed the German liner *St. Louis*, which in 1939 made a troubled voyage from Germany to Havana with 900 Jewish refugees aboard. The *Irpinia* was finally retired in 1981, by which time she was fifty-two years old. Two years later, she was broken up at La Spezia, as seen here. *Antonio Scrimali.*

Sidi-Ferruch, Sidi-Okba and Sidi-Mabrouk

In addition to their South American service, Transports Maritimes also had an interest in the North African trade. Just after the War, in 1947-49, they built a threesome of shapely 3,900-ton passenger and cargo ships, also equipped to carry livestock and Algerian wine. The *Sidi-Ferruch* was built in France, at Ateliers et Chantiers de Bretagne, and the other two by a British yard, J. Samuel White of Cowes. Each of them was of about 372 feet in length. Accommodations were divided between 60 First Class, 30 in

Cabin Class and just over 500 in Fourth Class. The *Sidi-Mabrouk* is shown here. The three sisters sailed for about fifteen years before declining trade caused their withdrawal. The *Sidi-Ferruch* and *Sidi-Mabrouk* went to the French Navy in 1964, becoming the *Médoc* and *Morvan*. The 17-knot *Sidi-Okba* was sold to Greek owners, Typaldos Lines, also in 1964. First renamed *Mediterranean II*, she was soon rebuilt for cruising as the

Electra. In her new guise, she had all-First Class accommodations for 344 passengers. Typaldos was disbanded in 1967, but it was not until 1974 that the *Electra* was sold to Solemare Shipping, the so-called Sol Lines, and renamed *Princess Sissy*. We see her here in this guise. A decade later, she grounded at Hvar on January 7th 1976 and subsequently sank. She was not refloated until April 5th. Badly damaged, she was towed to Split, where she was declared a total loss and broken up. *Hisashi Noma Collection and Michael Cassar.*

The *Médoc* (seen here, still as the *Sidi-Ferruch*) and the *Morvan* (ex-*Sidi-Mabrouk*) were fitted out by the French Navy as barrack and accommodation ships for maintenance of their nuclear base in Polynesia. Both vessels were struck from the active list in 1971 but were kept in reserve for some years before being scrapped. *V. H. Young and L. A. Sawyer.*

Sidi-Bel-Abbes

Built by Swan, Hunter & Wigham Richardson at Newcastle in 1948, this 5,226-ton ship was a twin sister to Cie Mixte's *Président de Cazalet.* Used in the Marseilles – North Africa service, she carried 95 passengers in First Class, 226 in Tourist and 582 in Fourth Class. Long and rather low, she was sold to Greek buyers, Hellenic Mediterranean Lines, in 1963 and was renamed *Apollonia.* She ran very successfully on the Venice to Haifa route via Piraeus. Laid up at the end of her career, she was renamed *Precious* for the delivery voyage to breakers at Alang in June 1988.

Andres Hernandez Collection and Alex Duncan.

Provence

When the *Provence* was built in the early 1950s, airlines had only a limited impact on global transport. Passenger ships were still by far the main way to cross the oceans and, for the most part, "getting there was still half the fun". Transports Maritimes' Provence plied the route to the East Coast of South America, from Marseilles to Rio de Janeiro, Santos, Montevideo and Buenos Aires. Her passenger lists ranged from rich merchants and South American aristocrats to migrant labourers and their
families. They were divided into four classes – from 139 First Class in upper deck splendor, 167 Tourist and 508 Third to 470 Fourth class travelling in near-steerage conditions in large dormitories.

Seen here at Swan, Hunter's Neptune yard at Newcastle-upon-Tyne on February 22nd 1951, the 15,889-ton ship was then the largest newly-built post-War French liner. Some of the final interior decorations were done by French workers who had been sent over especially. On February 18th 1954, she collided with the tanker *Saxonsea* while in the River Plate and was so badly damaged that she did not return to Marseilles for over ten months and then needed additional repairs for a further three months before resuming service. *Cronican-Arroyo Collection.*

In 1963, the 580-foot long *Provence* was sent to New York, where she is shown arriving for the first time, on July 4th. She sailed on 7-day voyages from New York to Bermuda and Nassau for the short-lived Caribbean Cruise Lines. Two years previously, her Mediterranean – South America sailings had been co-ordinated with those of Italy's Costa Line. *Moran Towing & Transportation Co.*

In 1965, the *Provence* was sold outright to Costa and was renamed *Enrico C.* She sailed on much the same route as before – Genoa and Marseilles to the East Coast of South America, but carrying far more Italian passengers. In the early 1970s, she became virtually a full-time cruise ship, except for positioning voyages between cruising seasons in the Mediterranean and along the South American coast. Her itineraries took her into the Black Sea, to the Aegean, West Africa, the Indian Ocean, the Amazon and even to Antarctica. In 1983, she was called *Enrico Costa* in line with a new Costa Line naming policy.
Antonio Scrimali.

In 1994, the *Enrico Costa* was sold to Star Cruises (now Mediterranean Shipping Cruises) and called *Symphony*. In this 1999 photograph taken at Valletta, she is seen on the right with a smoke deflector on her funnel. In front of her is one of her fleetmates, the *Rhapsody* (ex-*Cunard Princess*). It was an unusual meeting for the two ships, both of which sail Mediterranean waters in summer. *Michael Cassar.*

Bretagne

Unlike the *Provence*, the 16,335-ton *Bretagne* was built at St. Nazaire. She was completed in January 1952. She too ran between Marseilles and South America, but her passenger accommodations were arranged differently from those of her sister – 131 in First Class, 167 in Tourist, 606 in Third Class and 368 in all-dormitory Fourth. Passenger loads on the South American route began to decline, however, and in 1961 the *Bretagne* was sold to the Greek-flag Chandris Lines and refitted as a two-class ship – 150 First and 1,050 Tourist. Used mainly in a Southampton – Australia

migrant service via Suez, she nevertheless spent two summers on charter to the New York-based Caribbean Cruise Lines, sailing on 13-day Caribbean and later 7-day Bermuda-Bahamas cruises. *Alex Duncan.*

In 1962, the *Bretagne* was renamed *Brittany* by her new Chandris owners. It was expected that she would continue her divided pattern: Australian sailings and then, in summertime, American cruising. But on April 8th 1963, she was destroyed by a fire, sparked off by a welder's torch while she was lying at the Skaramanga shipyards near Piraeus. Burnt out, sunk and later declared a complete loss, she was salvaged, but only to be sold to Italian shipbreakers. She was delivered to them at La Spezia on March 31st 1964.
V. H. Young and L. A. Sawyer.

10

Club Med

Club Med 1 and Club Med 2

Encouraged, perhaps, by the success of the Windstar trio of sail-equipped cruise ships of 1986-88, Services et Transports – a French company, but with Bahamas registry – ordered two large, five-masted schooners. The 14,745-ton *Club Med 1*, launched at Le Havre as the *Lafayette*, was managed by Club Med, the well-known resort and hotel operator. Completed in December 1989, the 453-passenger ship (seen here) divided her time between summers in the western Mediterranean and then winters in the Caribbean. *Club Med 2* followed in the late summer of 1992 and was used in South Pacific service. There were rumors of two further sailing ships but financial problems led to the sale of *Club Med 1* to the Carnival group in the spring of 1997. Sold for $45 million, she has been refitted (with a reduced capacity of 312) as the *Windsurf* for Carnival's Windstar Cruises division. *Luís Miguel Correia.*

11
Other Tonnage

Paul Gaugin

Built by Chantiers de l'Atlantique at St. Nazaire, the specialty cruise ship *Paul Gaugin* was completed in the fall of 1997. She is shown here during a stopover at Port Everglades on her delivery cruise from France to the South Pacific via the Caribbean and Panama. The date was December 20th, 1997. The 19,170-ton, 318-passenger vessel, owned by Services & Transport and registered under the French flag, but at the remote islands of Wallis & Futuna, is run by Radisson Seven Seas Cruises in 7-day cruises out of Papeete on Tahiti. *Andres Hernandez.*

Mistral

The 1,250-passenger *Mistral* was christened in July 1999 at Chantiers de l'Atlantique, St. Nazaire by the wife of the captain of the French national soccer team. At 47,000 tons, the *Mistral* ranked as the largest French-flag passenger ship to be built since the *France* in the early 1960s. She was, however, intended for long-term lease to Greece's Festival Cruises for Mediterranean and Caribbean service. She has been immensely successful. As a result, at least two more ships will follow in her wake. Now being built by Chantiers de l'Atlantique, they will be 58,000-tonners and will be called *European Vision* and *European Dream*. Like the *Mistral*, they will fly the French flag. The three

ships constitute the first passenger vessel project to be paid for entirely in euros. Two larger liners at approximately 80,000 tons are rumored to follow. The total order would be worth $1 billion to the French. The 711-foot long *Mistral* is seen here during a promotional visit to Hamburg on June 30th 1999. *Frank Behling, Andres Hernandez Collection.*

Adriana

This ship was built as the *Aquarius* for the Hellenic Mediterranean Lines in 1972. She came from the United Shipyards at Perama and was not only the first new ship to be created purposely for Aegean cruising but was also the first cruise ship to be built in Greece. In 1987, she was sold to Jadrolinija, the famous Yugoslav shipping company and became the *Adriana*, sailing mainly in the Adriatic, usually from Venice. However, in 1998, she was sold to Marina Cruises and is operated by a French company, Plein Cap. She has been used for cruising round the European coasts and, recently, further afield. The 4,591-ton *Adriana*, seen here at

Copenhagen on July 11th 1993, has accommodations for 324 passengers.   *Ove Nielsen.*

Another French-owned cruise ship is the 3,500-ton *Le Levant*, a yacht-like vessel which carries only 90 passengers. Owned by Compagnie des Iles du Ponant and flying French colors, she cruises in the North American Great Lakes and along the St Lawrence in the summer, and to the Caribbean and South America at other times.

At least two other cruise ships are on charter to the French as we go to press. The 16,631-ton *Vincent Van Gogh* is the former Soviet *Gruziya* (later used briefly as *Odessa Sky* and then *Club I*) and is operated by Nouvelles Frontières. The 2,682-ton *Viking Bordeaux*, run by Viking Bordeaux Cruises, is the former German day excursion ship *Bremerhaven* which was later rebuilt as the Sun Line cruise ship *Stella Maris II*.

12
Postscript

The tradition of French passenger ships will continue, as will the art of building new liners. Following a rebirth with the 33,900-ton sisterships *Nieuw Amsterdam* and *Noordam* in 1983-84 and then advancing within three years to the 73,100-ton *Sovereign of the Seas*, at the time the largest cruise ship afloat, Chantiers de l'Atlantique remains one of the World's most noted shipyards for passenger ship construction. Their latest creations are a quartet of 91,000-tonners for Celebrity Cruises. The first of these, the *Millennium*, entered service in June 2000. Then there is the new *Seven Seas Mariner* being built for Radisson Seven Seas Cruises. In the future, although not yet definitely confirmed, is the order for the largest liner ever built, Cunard's 150,000-ton *Queen Mary 2*, due in 2003-04. Indeed, more is to be written on Passenger Liners French Style.

Bibliography

Bonsor, N. R. P. *North Atlantic Seaway.* Prescot, Lancashire: T. Stephenson & Sons, Ltd ., 1955.

Braynard, Frank O. & Miller, William H. *Fifty Famous Liners, Vols, 1-3.* Cambridge: Patrick Stephens, Ltd., 1982-87.

Cooke, Anthony. *Liners & Cruise Ships – 2.* London: Carmania Press, 2000.

Crowdy Michael and O'Donoghue, Kevin (editors). *Marine News.* Kendal, Cumbria: World Ship Society, 1965-2000.

Devol, George (editor). *Ocean & Cruise News.* Stamford, Connecticut: World Ocean & Cruise Society, 1980-97.

Dunn, Laurence. *Passenger Liners.* Southampton: Adlard Coles, Ltd. 1961.

Dunn, Laurence. *Passenger Liners* (2nd Edition). Southampton: Adlard Coles, Ltd. 1965.

Eisele, Peter and Rau, William (editors). *Steamboat Bill.* Providence, Rhode Island: Steamship Historical Society of America, Inc., 1965-2000.

Haws, Duncan. *Merchant Fleets: French Line.* Uckfield, East Sussex: TCL Publications, 1996.

Kalmbach Publishing Co. *Ships and Sailing.* Milwaukee, 1950-60.

Kludas, Arnold. *Great Passenger Ships of the World, Vols 1-5.* Cambridge: Patrick Stephens, Ltd., 1972-76.

Kludas, Arnold. *Great Passenger Ships of the World, Vol. 6.* Cambridge: Patrick Stephens, Ltd., 1986.

Kludas, Arnold. *Great Passenger Ships of the World Today.* Sparkford, Somerset: Patrick Stephens, Ltd., 1992.

Kludas, A rnold. *Great Passenger Ships of the World.* Hamburg: Koehlers Verlags GmbH, 1997.

Miller, William H. *The Last Atlantic Liners.* London: Conway Maritime Press, Ltd., 1985.

Miller, William H. *The Last Blue Water Liners.* London, Conway Maritime Press, Ltd., 1986.

Miller, William H. *Picture History of the French Line.* Mineola, New York: Dover Publications, Inc., 1997.

Molteni de Villermont, Claude. *Un Siècle de Paquebots Français Par La Carte Postale.* Le Touvet: Editions Marcel-Didier Vrac, 1995.

Smith, Eugene W. Passenger *Ships of the World Past and Present.* Boston: George H. Dean Company, 1963.

Transportation Guides, Inc. *Official Steamship Guide.* New York, 1937-63.

Index